40 HADITH FROM

Sunan abu Dawud

SHAHRUL HUSSAIN
& ZAHED FETTAH

Forty Hadith from Sunan Abū Dāwūd

First Published in 2023 by
THE ISLAMIC FOUNDATION

Distributed by
KUBE PUBLISHING LTD
Tel +44 (0)1530 249230
E-mail: info@kubepublishing.com
Website: www.kubepublishing.com

Author Shahrul Hussain & Zahed Fettah
Editor Umm Marwan Ibrahim
Cover Design Afreen Fazil (Jaryah Studios)
Arabic/English layout & design Nasir Cadir

A Cataloguing-in-Publication Data record for this book
is available from the British Library

ISBN 978-0-86037-955-3
eISBN 978-0-86037-904-9

Printed by Elma Basim, Turkey

Dedication

For Adnan and Dawud

Contents

Introduction

All praise is due to Allah, the Lord of the universe, the Most Merciful the Most Kind, the Master of the Day of Judgement. Peace and blessings be upon Muhammad ﷺ, the final Prophet of Allah, and upon his family and Companions.

Hadith is one of the most important institutions in Islam. It contains the teachings of the Prophet Muhammad ﷺ regarding all aspects of Islam. It is indispensable in order to attain the correct understanding of the religion, and without it, guidance is not possible. Therefore, it is essential for all Muslims to make an effort to understand and study Hadith, even if it is at a basic level.

Unfortunately, most of the works of Hadith literature available in English are long, detailed, and viewed as heavy reads by the general masses. As these are religious texts, it can be daunting for beginners to understand the subject. There are mainly two types of books about Hadith in English. While one type deals with the science of Hadith in terms of its historical phenomena as a vital Islamic institution, the other consists of thick volumes of English renditions of Hadith corpuses—both of which can put off beginners from reading and understanding Hadith.

This dilemma gave birth to the 'Forty Ahadith' project, in which we set out to compile a series of forty ahadith from each of the six canonical books of Hadith. The collection aims to educate people who wish to enjoy Hadith literature without delving too deep into its technicalities. The style and language used in these books is non-specialised and thereby accessible to readers of all levels and ages. As such, the collection is also ideal for new Muslims who wish to learn more about Hadith.

In this particular volume, we have selected forty ahadith from *Sunan Abū Dāwūd* in order to give the reader a flavour of the Hadith literature found within the *Sunan*. There is no particular reason for choosing the ahadith mentioned herein. However, each hadith will reflect a unique theme so as to touch upon various aspects of the Islamic teachings, such as:

- Manners and Etiquettes
- Character of a Muslim
- Exhortations and Admonitions
- Remembrance of Allah
- Knowledge and Action
- Beliefs

When selecting the forty ahadith for each book in the series, we made sure to avoid lengthy and elaborate narrations or those that dealt with complex legal and theological matters. Instead, you will find that the selected ahadith focus on character, spirituality, morals, manners and ethics, and that the accompanying explanations of the ahadith focus on highlighting these aspects.

Within this volume is a simple discussion of the theoretical parameters of praiseworthy characters every Muslim should aspire to achieve, supererogatory virtuous acts of worship, and the moral philosophy (in particular normative ethics) of these ahadith. It is hoped that this will open the doors for readers to enquire more about Hadith as an important source of revelation.

Finally, it is worth pointing out that the reason for compiling forty ahadith is due to the virtuous nature of 'forty' ahadith recorded in many traditions of the Prophet Muhammad ﷺ. It is related that Prophet Muhammad ﷺ said, 'Whoever memorises forty ahadith regarding the matters of religion, Allah will resurrect him on the Day of Judgement from among the group of jurists and scholars' (*Bayhaqī*). Although this hadith is weak in its authenticity, many scholars have strongly supported acting on weak ahadith, which solely speak about virtues of good deeds, for the sake of spirituality. What is of even more benefit is to memorise forty ahadith from *Sunan Abū Dāwūd*. The short ahadith in this compilation may help facilitate young learners and beginners to memorise the beloved Prophet's sayings, which would be a great achievement.

We would like to conclude by thanking everyone who has made this project possible, especially Br Haris Ahmad from Kube Publishing House for his support; without his help, this project would not have been possible. The people we are most indebted to are the patrons of the Ibn Rushd Centre of Excellence for Islamic Research. This work is dedicated to them and all those who support the advancement of knowledge and research.

Shahrul Hussain & Zahed Fettah
8th April 2019 / 3rd Sha'bān 1440

Acknowledgments

It would not be possible to accomplish this work without the support of many great people, too many to mention all of them by name. First and foremost, we thank our parents for their love and support. Our teachers without whom we would be nothing. We are most obliged to mention our heartfelt thanks to Abida Akhtar and Sumayah Ali for their invaluable feedback. A very special heartfelt thanks to Rabiya Dawood and Heba Malick for their fastidious editorial work.

The English language or indeed any other language does not afford a word to express our deepest gratitude to Br Rizvan Khalid for his support and help. We would like to thank Maroof Sethi, Johirul Islam, Mohammed Shakeeb, Mohammed Najeeb, Syed Ali and Zahir Hussain for their support and encouragement.

"I ask Allah to raise the rank of my parents and bless them in this life and the next, for they have encouraged me on my path of learning and seeking knowledge."

Zahed Fettah

A Brief Biography of Imam Abū Dāwūd

The great Imam of Hadith, Imam Abū Dāwūd Sulaymān ibn al-Ashʿath ibn Isḥāq al-Azdī al-Sijistānī was born in the year 202 AH in Sijistan, a town in the southwest of Afghanistan, on the borders of what is known today as Pakistan and Iran.

Imam Abū Dāwūd travelled to many lands seeking to study Hadith, initially travelling to Baghdad and Basra when he was only around 18 years of age. He also travelled to Khurasan, Iraq, the Arabian Peninsula, Sham (Levant) and Egypt. He narrated ahadith from some of the most senior scholars of Hadith in his time. His teachers include, ʿAbdullāh ibn Maslamah al-Qaʿnabī and Sulaymān ibn Harb in Makkah, Abū al-Walīd al-Ṭayālisī in Basra, Hishām ibn ʿAmmār in Damascus, and the great jurists and Hadith scholars Aḥmad ibn Ḥanbal and Isḥāq ibn Rāhwayh in Baghdad and Khurasan respectively. He was a particularly close student of Imam Aḥmad and compiled a collection of questions and answers directed at the imam. This compilation contains the opinions of Imam Aḥmad on matters pertaining to hadith, legal rulings, the authenticity and weakness of reports, and discussions on hadith narrators. He also often quotes Imam Aḥmad's explanations of the ahadith that he relates in his great work, the *Sunan*.

His students were some of the great scholars of Hadith too. The likes of Tirmidhī and Nasā'ī, both narrate ahadith from Abū Dāwūd in their works. Abū 'Awānah, al-Ājurrī and al-Dūlābī, three leading scholars of their time, were also from his students.

Aḥmad ibn Muḥammad al-Harawī said: 'Abū Dāwūd is from the vanguard of Hadith experts due to his knowledge of hadith, its defects, and chains of transmission. This is alongside his great level of worship, modesty, righteousness, and piety. He was one of the defenders and custodians of Hadith.' Imam Ḥākim al-Naysābūrī (d. 405 AH) said: 'Abū Dāwūd is the *imam* (leading scholar) of Ahl al-Hadith of his time without any comparison.'

Imam Abū Dāwūd authored some extremely important books, the two most important of them being, *Kitāb al-Sunan* and *Kitāb al-Marāsīl*. The first is considered arguably to be the greatest reference for the Prophet's ahadith, after *Ṣaḥīḥ al-Bukhārī* and *Ṣaḥīḥ Muslim*. It contains around 5,000 Prophetic reports which form the basis of the most important legal rulings and Islamic teachings. Imam Abū Dāwūd sent a letter to the people of Makkah explaining the objective behind authoring his book, the importance of the book, and his conditions for reporting any hadith in it. He explains that almost every important hadith is mentioned in his book, explicitly or through another hadith providing similar meanings. Throughout his book, he provides important comments about hadith authenticity and the meanings of hadith, making his work a comprehensive understanding of the Prophet Muhammad ﷺ and his teachings.

Imam Abū Dāwūd passed away in the year 275 AH in Basra, may Allah have mercy on him.

The Importance of Hadith and its Significance

Allah sent Messengers throughout history with the objective of clarifying the truth to the people and guiding them to Him. Many of these Messengers were also sent with Books containing guidance, such as the final Messenger of Allah, Prophet Muhammad ﷺ. He was sent to teach the Book, the Qur'an, and to be the living example of the teachings of the Qur'an. As Allah states in the Qur'an: *'Allah has surely conferred a favour on the believers when He sent in their midst a Messenger from among themselves who recites to them His verses, purifies them, and teaches them the Book and the Wisdom, while previously they had been in clear misguidance'* (Āl 'Imrān 3: 164). Allah also states: *'And we have sent down the Reminder (the Qur'an) to you so that you (O Messenger) may clarify to the people that which has been sent down to them, and so that they may ponder'* (al-Naḥl 16: 44).

These verses highlight that the role of the Messenger ﷺ is to clarify and teach the Qur'an. His words and his actions, which form a verbal and practical interpretation of the Qur'an, is the Prophetic Tradition referred to as the 'Sunnah'. Following the Sunnah is necessary because it is the only way to practice the teachings of the final Book of Allah correctly.

Allah has taken it upon Himself to preserve the Qur'an: *'It is certainly We who have revealed the Reminder, and it is certainly We who will preserve it'* (al-Ḥijr 15: 9). This preservation is not restricted to the letters and words of the Qur'an but also includes the preservation of its meanings, which is fulfilled through the Prophetic implementation of the Qur'an—the Sunnah.

It is simply not possible to observe the teachings of Islam without following the Sunnah. The purpose of the Qur'an is to teach us the correct belief and acts of worship Allah demands from us in order to prove our servitude to Him. It is not, however, an instruction manual detailing precise rules and methods of worshipping Allah.

Moreover, written or verbal instructions are not enough; it requires a teacher to show us the practical way of worshipping Allah. Thus, while the Qur'an outlines the commandments of Allah such as to fast, give zakat, perform hajj and the like, the role of the Prophet ﷺ is to teach us *how* to perform those acts of worship. Therefore, without knowing and following the Sunnah, Muslims will not be able to observe the teachings of the Qur'an.

Compilation of Hadith

Although the Qur'an was collected and written in one place much earlier than the Hadith, the latter was also preserved in similar ways to the former. Ahadith were written down by some Companions at the time of the Messenger ﷺ, but this habit only became widespread a century or so after his death.

Since the second century after *hijrah*, many scholars wrote down the ahadith of the Prophet ﷺ. Some scholars compiled books of Hadith which discussed the various areas of the teachings of the Prophet ﷺ. Sadly, some of the earliest books of Hadith were lost. However, some survived and were transmitted throughout centuries until our time, including the *Muwaṭṭā'* of Imam Mālik (d. 179 AH), the *Muṣannaf* of 'Abd al-Razzāq (d. 211 AH), the *Muṣannaf* of Ibn Abī Shaybah (d. 235 AH), and the *Musnad* of Imam Aḥmad ibn Ḥanbal (d. 241 AH). These books contain thousands of reports from the Prophet ﷺ and his Companions, clarifying how they implemented the Qur'anic teachings in their everyday life.

Hundreds of books of Hadith were authored, but only a dozen of them became famous and spread worldwide. The nine most relied-upon books of Hadith are:

1. *Ṣaḥīḥ al-Bukhārī*
2. *Ṣaḥīḥ Muslim*
3. *Sunan Abū Dāwūd*
4. *Sunan al-Tirmidhī*
5. *Sunan al-Nasā'ī*
6. *Sunan Ibn Mājah*
7. *Muwaṭṭa' Mālik*

8. *Musnad Aḥmad*
9. *Musnad al- Dārimī*

The Classification of Hadith

In the early generations, during the time of the Companions of the Prophet, it was quite easy to know the Sunnah of the Prophet ﷺ because the Companions had witnessed him directly. Unfortunately, in the generations that followed, some people would make false attributions to the Prophet ﷺ and claim that he said things which he had not said. They would do this with different intentions and agendas. This led to the scholars of Hadith putting an impressive amount of effort into preserving the Sunnah and distinguishing between authentic reports and false ones. They would study chains of narrations, the biographies of hadith narrators, and the texts of hadith in order to conclude which reports can comfortably be attributed to the Prophet ﷺ. Volumes have been written about those who narrated hadith so that we are able to know who the reliable and unreliable transmitters of hadith are. This effort was a collective one by many of the greatest scholars of Hadith, ensuring that the Sunnah of the Prophet ﷺ was preserved so that the Muslims may act upon it as Allah commanded them in the Qur'an.

This effort to study the Prophetic Traditions resulted in the formation of the science of Hadith. This became one of the most important of the Islamic sciences. It discusses chains of narration, different types of ahadith, the conditions for an authentic hadith, the different methods of transmitting hadith, the *fiqh* (understanding) of ahadith, and other relevant areas. Separate books have been authored in this science, known as *uṣūl al-ḥadīth* or *muṣṭalaḥ al-ḥadīth*, from the fourth century onwards. Some prominent works in this field include, *Maʿrifat ʿUlūm al-Ḥadīth* by Ḥākim al-Naysābūrī (d. 405 AH) and *Maʿrifat Anwāʿ ʿUlūm al-Ḥadīth* by Imam Abū ʿAmr ibn al-Ṣalāḥ (d. 643 AH).

Studying the sciences of Hadith is an essential part of Islamic studies. We can only understand the Qur'an and the Shariah if we have a strong grounding in the sciences of Hadith and a good understanding of the *fiqh* of Hadith.

However, Hadith studies is usually a subject for the most dedicated of learners because it requires attention to detail. For instance, there are many classifications and categories of Hadith. Advanced readers can refer to the *Muqaddimah* by Ibn Ṣalāḥ which is also available in English. Readers who have access to Arabic can refer to many resources such as *al-Irshād* by al-Nawawī (which he later summarised in his *Taqrīb*), al-Suyūṭī's *Tadrīb al-Rāwī*, Ibn Kathīr's *Ikhtiṣār 'Ulūm al-Ḥadīth*, al-Zarkashī's *al-Nukat*, al-'Iraqi's *al-Taqyīd wa al-Īḍāḥ* and Ibn Ḥajar al-'Asqalānī's *Nukhbat al-Fikr*.

As a beginner, you should know that scholars have made four major classifications of hadith based on the soundness of the hadith in terms of the reliability and memory of its reporters:

1. *Ṣaḥīḥ* (rigorously authentic)
2. *Ḥasan* (good)
3. *Ḍaʿīf* (weak)
4. *Mawḍūʿ* (fabricated)

Ṣaḥīḥ (rigorously authentic)

This is defined by Ibn Ṣalāḥ as a hadith which has a continuous chain of narrators (*isnād*), who have narrated the hadith from only trustworthy (*thiqah*) narrators (those with perfect memory and uprightness) and it (the hadith) is free from irregularities (in the text) and defects (in the *isnād*). Such as: Mālik—from Nāfiʿ—from 'Abdullāh ibn Umar.

Ḥasan (good)

Al-Tirmidhī defines *ḥasan* as a hadith which is not irregular (*shādh*) nor contains a disparaged reporter in its chain of narrators, and is reported through more than one channel. Examples of *ḥasan* ahadith are those which have been reported by: 'Amr ibn Shu'ayb—from his father—from his grandfather or Muḥammad ibn 'Amr—from Abū Salamah—from Abū Hurayrah.

Ḍa'īf (weak)

A weak hadith is a hadith which has failed to meet the standard of ṣaḥīḥ or ḥasan. It is usually one that has faults in the continuity of the chain of narrators (isnād) or has a fault in a narrator in terms of lack of reliability either in memory or uprightness.

Mawḍū' (fabricated)

These are ahadith which the Prophet Muhammad ﷺ never said, but due to personal motives, were fabricated and attributed to him. A fabricated hadith can be detected either because one of the narrators is known to be a liar or because the text is of an obnoxious nature, thus going against the principles of Islam. For example, it is (falsely) attributed to the Prophet Muhammad ﷺ that he said, 'A negro will fornicate when his belly is full and steal when he is hungry.' This is fabricated due to its obnoxious nature, hence going against the noble character of the Prophet Muhammad ﷺ.

Oftentimes though, the wordings of a fabricated hadith may be non-offensive or even sound sensible. For example, 'To return one dāniq (a sixth of a dirham) to its owner is better than worshipping (Allah) for seventy years.' At such instances, scrutinising the hadith based on the thoroughly developed science of hadith classification would help us determine if it was in fact narrated by the Prophet Muhammad ﷺ or simply made up and falsely attributed to him.

Being Compassionate to Allah's Creation

عَنْ عَبْدِ اللَّهِ بْنِ عَمْرٍو يَبْلُغُ بِهِ النَّبِيَّ ﷺ الرَّاحِمُونَ يَرْحَمُهُمُ
الرَّحْمَنُ ارْحَمُوا أَهْلَ الأَرْضِ يَرْحَمْكُمْ مَنْ فِي السَّمَاءِ

'Abdullāh ibn 'Amr ibn al-'Āṣ ﷺ narrated that the
Prophet ﷺ said: 'Allah is merciful to those who are
merciful. Show mercy to those who are on the Earth, and
He who is in the Heaven will show mercy to you.'

Mercy and compassion are key adjectives to describe Allah's relationship towards His creation. Allah describes Himself as *al-Raḥmān*, the Beneficent, and He has made mercy and compassion obligatory upon Himself. Allah commands us to remember this, which we do so by reciting the Divine words that talk about Him being the Most Merciful and Most Kind many times in our daily lives as well as in the five daily prayers. In fact, we say these words more than any other phrase in Islam, which signifies the high level of importance of Allah's mercy and compassion. We say *bismillāh al-raḥmān al-raḥīm* (In the name of Allah the Most Merciful the Most Kind) many times in our daily lives to help reinforce in our minds these qualities of Allah.

We can witness mercy and compassion being exercised within the creation of Allah, be they humans or animals. A mother is always protective of her offspring and mindful of their safety. She will go to great lengths to provide food for them, give them shelter and keep them out of harm's way. It is Allah who has taught His creation to bear this attribute of mercy.

This hadith teaches us the moral obligation of being compassionate, caring and mindful of not harming any of God's creation unless there is a need. Let us take an example of a lion or any other predator that kills other animals for food; it will only kill that which it needs to survive and does not kill for the sake of fun and sport. Being conscious of the environment and the ecosystem, and not harming it in any way is a part of the teachings of Islam. If we fail to be conscious of our environment and harm other creatures who share the same space as we do, it will only result in Allah taking away His mercy from us. However, if we show care and compassion to everything around us, we will have Allah and His angels in the Heavens showing us mercy. Being cruel to any of Allah's creation will cause the displeasure of Allah and take us away from His mercy.

Order and Discipline Create Harmony

عَنْ أَبِى هُرَيْرَةَ عَنْ رَسُولِ اللَّهِ ﷺ قَالَ إِذَا صَلَّى أَحَدُكُمْ فَخَلَعَ
نَعْلَيْهِ فَلاَ يُؤْذِ بِهِمَا أَحَدًا لِيَجْعَلْهُمَا بَيْنَ رِجْلَيْهِ أَوْ لِيُصَلِّ فِيهِمَا

Abū Hurayrah ﷺ reported the Messenger of Allah ﷺ as
saying: 'When any of you attends prayer and takes off his
sandals, he should not harm anyone by them. He should
place them between his feet or pray with them on.'

The teachings of the Prophet Muhammad ﷺ consistently talk
about avoiding harm to others. Not only should a person avoid
harming others, but they should avoid harming themself, too. Eating
or drinking harmful substances, being friends with bad people, being
detached from the worship of Allah are few examples of harming
oneself. However, when we harm ourself the harm is restricted to
affecting one particular individual, but when the harm is broadened
and brought into the public sphere and others are affected, that action
becomes a matter of public concern.

Perhaps more than ever before, we can see the problem with people who go to the mosques, take off their shoes and leave them on the floor without any regard for others. The lack of concern over the harm it may cause others in terms of it being an obstacle for easy entrance to and exit from the mosque can be disappointing. Almost all mosques have a dedicated area to store the shoes, yet many mosque users are neglectful and, either out of laziness or simply indifference, they leave their shoes on the floor, making the mosque entrance untidy and hazardous. In the modern world the same principle can be applied to the way we park our cars to go to the mosque. When we are careless and park our cars in the wrong places, it will cause other people a lot of problems.

This hadith teaches us many lessons. The first and foremost is that doing anything which may cause harm to others is not acceptable. We may think that our petty actions are just that—petty and minor—yet to others it may cause great harm. The hadith teaches us to be mindful and think whether or not what we are doing may disrupt others and harm them.

This hadith also teaches us the importance of personal responsibility which is required to create an atmosphere of order and discipline. A simple act of removing shoes and putting them in the correct place represents fulfilling one's personal responsibility of not harming others and one's self-discipline of keeping things where they ought to be. If every person were to be considerate enough to ensure that he or she is not harming anyone and disciplined enough to place items in their rightful place, then this will have such a powerful impact on society and the world at large.

From the aspect of legal rulings, this hadith teaches us that if the shoes are clean, they can be brought into the mosque and the same applies to other personal belongings. The permissibility of praying with shoes on is also established by this hadith as is the permissibility of entering the mosque with shoes on. However, this must be understood in the context of its time. The mosque of the Prophet ﷺ did not have carpet or any other flooring, save the natural earth. Therefore, wearing shoes into the mosque was not much of an issue. Nowadays mosques have carpets, and bringing outdoor shoes can make the carpet dirty and unclean which will cause many people discomfort. This is why the common practice all over the Muslim world is not to wear shoes inside the mosque.

Suitable Places for Prayer

وَعَنْ أَبِي سَعِيدٍ ﴾ أَنَّ النَّبِيَّ ﴿ قَالَ الْأَرْضُ كُلُّهَا مَسْجِدٌ إِلاَّ

الْحَمَّامَ وَالْمَقْبَرَةَ

Abu Sa'id al-Khudri ﴿ reported that the Prophet ﴾ said:
'The whole earth is a place of prayer except public baths
and graveyards.'

Islam teaches us that Allah did not need to bring any creature
into existence, but He did, and He did it for the purpose of them
worshipping Him. Allah gave some creatures free will and left it up to
them to either choose to worship Him or disobey Him, whereas for
some creatures, He did not give them that choice. There are rules and
methods of worshipping Allah, and these rules differed from prophet
to prophet. Some of the previous religious communities received strict
rules of where and how to worship Allah while other communities
were given lenient rules.

For Muslims, any good action, no matter how small, if done for the sake of Allah, is considered an act of worship. Of course, there are some formal acts of worship which have procedures, conditions and methods of execution which must be observed in a particular manner. These are acts of worship such as the prayer (ṣalāh), fasting, zakat, hajj and the like. Unlike other acts of worship mentioned, ṣalāh is the only one which must be offered daily and several times a day. The five daily prayers are a crucial part of a Muslim's daily activity. It is what connects us to Allah and constantly reminds us about His Oneness and the purpose of why we were created. The word ṣalāh is not only connected to the five compulsory prayers of the day but also includes extra voluntary acts of prayer.

Human life can be a very busy affair, and at times it happens that we do not have a moment to spare. Allah was lenient to the followers of the Prophet Muhammad ﷺ and in order to make our lives easier Allah has made prayer valid in any part of the world. It was a special favour granted to the Prophet Muhammad ﷺ that the entire earth is a source of purification and a suitable place for prayer for him and his followers. This provision has been made so that no excuse can be given for not praying when the time for prayer has commenced.

Although prayer is valid at any place which is pure, there are however, two places which are disapproved: public baths and graveyards. The reason why they are disapproved is because these places are generally not considered the best places in terms of hygiene. No one would want to have a meal at a public bath or a graveyard because these places are regarded as impure and unpleasant. The environment a person is in plays an important part in their attitude. Since prayer must be done with concentration and devotion, being in a place such as the public bath, which is unclean, or the graveyard, which is dull and grim, is not conducive to create that atmosphere. This is one of the reasons why these two places are disapproved places for prayer.

Islam Teaches us Everything

عَنْ سَلْمَانَ قَالَ قِيلَ لَهُ لَقَدْ عَلَّمَكُمْ نَبِيُّكُمْ كُلَّ شَىْءٍ حَتَّى
الْخِرَاءَةَ قَالَ أَجَلْ لَقَدْ نَهَانَا صلى الله عليه وسلم أَنْ نَسْتَقْبِلَ
الْقِبْلَةَ بِغَائِطٍ أَوْ بَوْلٍ وَأَنْ لاَ نَسْتَنْجِىَ بِالْيَمِينِ وَأَنْ لاَ يَسْتَنْجِىَ
أَحَدُنَا بِأَقَلَّ مِنْ ثَلاَثَةِ أَحْجَارٍ أَوْ يَسْتَنْجِىَ بِرَجِيعٍ أَوْ عَظْمٍ

Salmān al-Fārisī ﷺ narrated that someone said to him:
'Your prophet teaches you everything, even about using
the toilet?' Salmān al-Fārisī replied: 'Yes. He has forbidden
us to face the *qiblah* at the time of defecating or urinating,
and cleansing with right hand, and cleansing with less
than three stones, or cleansing with dung or bones.'

One of the unique features of the religion of Islam is the level of
detail provided on how to live our daily lives and how to conduct
ourselves. The Prophet Muhammad ﷺ spent a lot of time teaching his

Companions many aspects of life, from the basics of personal hygiene to complicated issues such as good governance and international relationships. The detailed teachings of the Prophet Muhammad ﷺ were noticed even by the non-Muslim community of his time. Once, some non-Muslims came to the great Persian Companion Salmān al-Fārisī ؓ, and said to him in an inquisitive way that they heard that the Prophet Muhammad ﷺ teaches his followers about all aspects of life including something as trivial as using the toilet, and they wanted to know if that was true. The Prophet's Companion, Salmān al-Fārisī ؓ, replied in the affirmative and informed them that the Prophet Muhammad ﷺ taught them about the etiquettes of using the privy. The Prophet Muhammad ﷺ gave Muslims four instructions of what not to do during the process of relieving oneself.

The Kaaba is one of the most sacred monuments in Islam. Facing towards it during the process of relieving oneself is seen as an act of disrespect and therefore, should be avoided. The right hand is used for many things such as eating, writing, handling things, shaking hands and the like. It is therefore offensive to use the same hand for cleaning oneself after using the toilet as well. Being thorough in cleaning oneself is vitally important and Islam deals quite harshly with people who are neglectful in this respect, by warning them of severe punishments in the grave due to it.[1] To make sure that hygiene has been achieved, the Prophet Muhammad ﷺ instructed Muslims to use a minimum of three wiping agents. During the Prophet's time, people would use stones as an object to remove filth. Of course, the optimal method is to wipe and wash to ensure the complete removal of filth.

Apart from the vital lessons of personal hygiene this hadith teaches, it also provides us with one very important piece of information: Allah and His Messenger ﷺ have taught us everything we need to know to live our lives. This is why we find ahadith that

---

1   Abu Dawud, *Sunan Abu Dawud*, Hadith no. 20

discuss a myriad of topics such as personal hygiene, prayer, charity, spirituality, marriage, divorce, criminal law, judgeship, leadership, parenting skills and so much more. The Sunnah truly does cover all aspects of our lives, and where direct instructions do not exist to a problem, we have enough guidelines to work out the solution. This is a truly beautiful and unique aspect of Islam.

The Etiquettes of
Leaving the Toilet

عَنْ عَائِشَةَ ﷺ أَنَّ النَّبِيَّ ﷺ كَانَ إِذَا خَرَجَ
مِنَ الْغَائِطِ قَالَ غُفْرَانَكَ

'Āʾishah ﷺ narrated that when the Prophet ﷺ came out
of the privy, he used to say: 'Grant me your forgiveness.'

Remembering Allah should be a daily feature of our lives and we
should try to engage in His remembrance as much as possible.
Remembering Allah represents our gratitude to Allah, and gratitude
is not only due during good times but during tough times as well.
In fact, the real test of a person's gratefulness lies in their response to
the hardships they face. The previous hadith demonstrated that the
Prophet Muhammad ﷺ has taught us all that we need to know about
the various aspects of our lives, including what not to do during the
process of relieving ourselves. In this hadith, the Prophet ﷺ explains
to us what to do *after* relieving ourselves. He taught us that a person
should cover himself or herself upon leaving the designated toilet area
and should say, '*Ghufrānak*' (O Allah, grant me your forgiveness).

This hadith reinforces the fact that the Prophet Muhammad ﷺ did indeed teach us the minute details of life. It also shows us that he thanked Allah on every occasion. Human physiology demands that we must consume food and water in order to survive. Human life depends on the intake of food, but this is only the first part of the process of our survival. The most important part of eating is what the body does with the food. The complex process of how the body deals with food is a miracle in itself and a testament to the Majesty of Allah. The intake of food and water requires that after the body has processed the food and supplied the body with the nutrients it has extracted from the food, the leftover needs to be discarded. However, if in this complex process of extracting nutrients and supplying it to the body, of storing excess energy and of separating the good from the bad, there happens to be a malfunction, then its consequences can be devastating if not catastrophic. It is by the grace of Allah that we experience the process of food and water with great ease, and therefore it behoves that we should be thankful to Allah. Since thankfulness to Allah includes His remembrance and asking Him for His forgiveness, we are guided to say '*Ghufrānak*' when exiting the toilet. By copying the Prophet Muhammad ﷺ in practising this simple act from his Sunnah, we can easily get closer to Allah, attain His pleasure and achieve the happiness of both worlds.

The Importance of Suḥūr

عَنْ عَمْرِو بْنِ الْعَاصِ ﷺ قَالَ قَالَ رَسُولُ اللَّهِ ﷺ إِنَّ فَضْلَ مَا
بَيْنَ صِيَامِنَا وَصِيَامِ أَهْلِ الْكِتَابِ أَكْلَةُ السَّحَرِ

'Amr ibn al-'Āṣ ﷺ narrates the Messenger of Allah ﷺ as saying: 'The difference between our fasting and that of the People of the Book is eating the pre-dawn meal.'

One of the greatest honours for Muslims is that they are the followers of the greatest prophet and greatest man ever to walk the Earth—Prophet Muhammad ﷺ. He is described as the 'best of creation' (*ashraf al-makhlūqāt*), ranked as the perfect human being and the most beloved to Allah Most High. Every prophet was sent to his community to teach the people about the worship of One God, the laws of God and ethics and morality. Details of what previous communities received about how to worship Allah have been lost, and only some information about the rituals of the Jewish and Christian communities is still available today. However, Islam contests the accuracy of some of the teachings of Judaism and Christianity, because it asserts that the Jews and Christians changed some of the teaching of their prophet after a period of time.

What Islam shares in common with other faiths is the requirement of performing spiritual acts of worship. Islam contains some acts of worship similar to those of Judaism and Christianity in particular, and others completely different from them. For example, *ṣalāh* or prayer is distinctly different from the way Jews and Christians worship God. Although differing in details, alms (zakat) is a common institution Islam shares with Judaism and Christianity. Fasting is another example of an act of worship that Muslims have in common with other members of the Abrahamic faith. Allah says in the Qur'an: *'O you who believe, fasting has been set for you as it was set for those before you so that you may learn to fear Allah'* (*al-Baqarah* 2: 183). Fasting requires giving up food and water for the sake of Allah. It symbolises an act of sacrifice a person completes purely to please Him.

Although there may be some shared ritual acts of worship with members of other religions, Islam was very keen on establishing a distinct identity for its followers, and to this end the Prophet Muhammad ﷺ consistently taught his followers that if there was an overlap with Judaic or Christian practices then there must be something to set Muslims apart from members of other religious communities. Since both Jews and Christians fast, the Prophet Muhammad ﷺ taught Muslims to be different from them by having a pre-dawn meal known as *suḥūr*. Although *suḥūr* is not a prerequisite to fasting, it is full of blessings from Allah. Having the *suḥūr* will provide the fasting person with a significant supply of energy, which they will need in order to go through the day. This will help the body deal with fasting a lot better.

The most important thing we must learn from this hadith is to inculcate the good practice of having *suḥūr* and that as Muslims, we must incline to be distinct in our ways of worshipping Allah from other religious communities. It is important to note that this does not mean that Muslims cannot be friends with members of other faiths; it simply means that Islamic acts of worship must be different from other faith communities.

❦

7

It is Natural to Cry for Someone who has Died

عَنْ أَنَسِ بْنِ مَالِكٍ ﷺ قَالَ قَالَ رَسُولُ اللَّهِ ﷺ وُلِدَ لِيَ اللَّيْلَةَ غُلاَمٌ فَسَمَّيْتُهُ بِاسْمِ أَبِي إِبْرَاهِيمَ قَالَ أَنَسٌ لَقَدْ رَأَيْتُهُ يَكِيدُ بِنَفْسِهِ بَيْنَ يَدَىْ رَسُولِ اللَّهِ ﷺ فَدَمَعَتْ عَيْنَا رَسُولِ اللَّهِ ﷺ فَقَالَ تَدْمَعُ الْعَيْنُ وَيَحْزَنُ الْقَلْبُ وَلاَ نَقُولُ إِلاَّ مَا يَرْضَى رَبُّنَا إِنَّا بِكَ يَا إِبْرَاهِيمُ لَمَحْزُونُونَ

Anas ibn Mālik ﷺ narrated the Messenger of Allah ﷺ as saying: 'A child was born to me at night and I named him Ibrahim after my (fore)father.' Anas said: 'I saw it at the point of death before the Messenger of Allah. Tears began to fall from the eyes of the Messenger of Allah. He said: "The eye weeps and the heart grieves, but we say only what our Lord is pleased with; and we are grieved for you, O Ibrahim.'"

The best role model for us is the Prophet Muhammad ﷺ. He has taught us what polite behaviour is, what dignified manners look like, and how we must conduct ourselves in all circumstances and at all times. Before prophethood, Allah blessed the Prophet Muhammad ﷺ with six children, four girls and two boys, with his first wife Khadijah bint Khuwaylid ؓ. The two boys died during infancy and the girls lived to adulthood. The Prophet Muhammad ﷺ loved children. Sometimes if he found children on the road playing, he would play with them. He loved his daughter Fatima ؓ and loved her two children Hasan and Hussain ؓ even more. When the Prophet ﷺ was slightly advanced in age, Allah blessed him with another boy through his wife Māriyah al-Qibṭiyyah ؓ. The Prophet ﷺ was delighted with his child and named him Ibrahīm after his ancestor, Prophet Ibrahīm ؑ. Unfortunately, Ibrahīm ibn Muhammad did not live too long. Some historians say that he only lived 16-18 months before he fell seriously ill. It was the will of Allah that Ibrahīm could not recover from his illness and passed away while being cradled by his father, the Prophet ﷺ.

There are some very important lessons we can learn from this hadith. Many people struggle to deal with the death of their infant children and some question why it had to happen to them. We must understand that Allah takes lives only because He is the giver of life and death, and that life and death happen at His will. By no means does it imply that He is displeased with anyone. This is what Allah wanted to teach people when He chose to take away the beloved son of the Prophet Muhammad ﷺ himself.

Look at the response of the Prophet Muhammad ﷺ when his son died in his arms. The Prophet ﷺ did not wail, scream or shout. He cried as a natural response to sad news, and even at the time of great grief, he continued to teach right mannerism, decorum and code of conduct. During such sad news many people fall victim to immense grief. They lose their sense of dignity and end up uttering inappropriate words. It is this scenario the Prophet Muhammad ﷺ wanted to give a piece of advice about when he said: 'The eye weeps and the heart grieves, but we say only what our Lord is pleased with, and we are grieved for you, O Ibrahīm.' It is important at the time of receiving devastating news that people remain composed and careful not to utter inappropriate words. Inappropriate actions are also blameworthy. At the time of someone's death, some people wail and scream out of grief. This is prohibited in Islam. Natural outbursts of tears and sounds of crying are normal and acceptable but raised voices and wailing must be avoided at all costs.

8

Praying for the Dead

عَنْ أَبِي هُرَيْرَةَ ﷺ قَالَ سَمِعْتُ رَسُولَ اللهِ ﷺ يَقُولُ إِذَا صَلَّيْتُمْ
عَلَى الْمَيِّتِ فَأَخْلِصُوا لَهُ الدُّعَاءَ

Abū Hurayrah ﷺ narrated that the Prophet ﷺ said:
'When you pray over the dead, make a sincere supplication
for him.'

Death is an inevitable and inescapable part of life. It gives
perspective to the meaning and purpose of life in the sense that
because we know that our lives will come to an end, we know that we
must live a good life on Earth in order for us to have a better life in
the Hereafter. Allah says in the Qur'an: *'Blessed is He in whose Hand
is the dominion of the Universe, and who has power over everything. He
who created death and life that He might test you as to which of you is
best in good deeds'* (*al-Mulk* 67: 1–2). There was no need for Allah to
create us, but He did, and the reason why He created us is so that we
worship Him.

Allah has therefore given us the opportunity to worship Him and do good deeds by observing His commandments and avoiding what He has declared unlawful. Life on Earth is the place a person must strive to attain closeness with Allah, seek His pleasure and earn His forgiveness. A person who has managed to do all this is indeed the successful one.

There is only one difficulty with this: How do we know that Allah has forgiven us, granted us His pleasure and taken us close to Him? The answer is of course that we don't know for sure. No one can be certain that Allah has forgiven them no matter how pious a person may seem, or how many mosques, schools and hospitals they have built for the poor. Our salvation is only known by Allah, but what we can do is hope that Allah has accepted our deeds because we were sincere in what we did.

The opportunity to do good deeds is therefore limited to life on Earth but when a person passes away the living can help them in a handful of ways. One of these ways is by making *du'ā'* or supplication for them.

In this hadith, the Prophet ﷺ taught us to make sincere supplication for the deceased, during the funeral prayer, asking Allah to forgive them and grant them Paradise. Making *du'ā'* for our dead is the best way to show that we appreciated them and what they did for us in life; it is the best way to show that we loved them and continue to do so.

Praying for the dead does not stop at the point of burial. There are several things we can do to pray for the deceased. For example, we can posthumously make a charitable donation in their name. After our prayers when we make our supplication to Allah, we can ask Him to grant the dead a smooth journey to the Hereafter especially during their stay at the grave known as the *barzakh* period. Some scholars like Hanafi and Hanbali jurists encourage people to recite Qur'an for the deceased.[2] One of the most important things we can do is ask Allah to forgive them for any of their shortcomings or even their transgressions against us or others. Letting go of any wrong they have done to you is a great way of praying for the dead. It is an act of mercy and kindness which will be shown back to you by Allah, Most High, in the way of forgiving you when you most need it.

It is equally important for us to pray for someone who has passed away and we have wronged them but failed to apologise for it while they were alive and attain their forgiveness. Now that they are dead it is no longer possible to ask them to forgive you, but you can make up for this error by praying for them. Your *du'ā's* will act as atonement for your shortcomings.

Remembering the deceased in a positive manner is a form of making *du'ā* for him/her and mentioning them in a bad way is a way of harming them. Hence, if you don't have anything good to say about the deceased then you should not say anything. They are with Allah, so leave it to Him to take care of them.

꧁꧂

---

2   Hussain, Shahrul, *What the Living Can do for the Dead,* White Thread Press, p. 84

9

Three Types of Judges

عَنِ ابْنِ بُرَيْدَةَ عَنْ أَبِيهِ ﷺ عَنِ النَّبِيّ ﷺ قَالَ الْقُضَاةُ ثَلَاثَةٌ
وَاحِدٌ فِي الْجَنَّةِ وَاثْنَانِ فِي النَّارِ فَأَمَّا الَّذِى فِي الْجَنَّةِ فَرَجُلٌ عَرَفَ
الْحَقَّ فَقَضَى بِهِ وَرَجُلٌ عَرَفَ الْحَقَّ فَجَارَ فِي الْحُكْمِ فَهُوَ فِي النَّارِ
وَرَجُلٌ قَضَى لِلنَّاسِ عَلَى جَهْلٍ فَهُوَ فِي النَّارِ

Buraydah ibn al-Ḥuṣayb ﷺ narrated that the Prophet ﷺ
said: 'Judges are of three types, one of whom will go to
Paradise and two to Hell. The one who will go to Paradise
is a man who knows what is right and gives judgement
accordingly; but a man who knows what is right and acts
tyrannically in his judgement will go to Hell; and a man
who gives judgement for people when he is ignorant will
go to Hell.'

Three Types of Judges

Having disagreements and disputes is unfortunately a part of human life and it is unavoidable. When a disagreement happens and it cannot be solved internally then there is a need to get a third person involved to listen to the case and the arguments and consider the evidence from both parties so that a judgement can be attained. Judgeship is a very important institution in Islam, and it comes with a serious station. Judges are the most powerful people in the country, even more powerful than the caliph or head of state. If people have a dispute with the caliph, they have the right to take him to court and seek judgement against him. The opinion of the judge is final, and the life and wealth of a person can depend on what a judge has to say.

Therefore, judgeship is indeed a serious position—one of great power and authority. Due to the serious nature of this post, there are strict guidelines and a code of conduct judges must adhere to in order for fairness and justice to be established. Unfortunately, corrupt and incompetent judges will always slip through the net, which is why the Prophet Muhammad ﷺ gave a stark warning to corrupt, incompetent and charlatan judges. Playing with people's lives is no laughing matter and only those who know themselves to be competent to hold the post of judgeship and will not allow power and corruption to get to them should apply for this post.

In another hadith, the Prophet Muhammad ﷺ talks about the serious nature of judgeship saying that a person who has been appointed as a judge has been slaughtered without a knife.[3] In other words, the Prophet ﷺ is asking the one who chooses to be a judge to be careful and ask themself if they really are capable of being a judge, if they possesses the correct skills, and if they can avoid the temptation of corruption.

In this hadith, the Prophet ﷺ talks about three types of judges: one of whom will go to Paradise, and the other two to Hell. The judge who will go to Paradise is the competent judge who has all the

---

3   Abu Dawud, *Sunan Abu Dawud*, Hadith no. 3572

necessary knowledge, skill and composure to hold the office of a judge. Consequently, they judge according to the Book of Allah and the Sunnah of His Messenger ﷺ.

The second type of judge the Prophet ﷺ talks about is a judge who is competent in terms of having the necessary knowledge and skill, but the power of their authority gets to their head and they judge with unfairness, excessive harshness and cruelty. The Prophet ﷺ said that such a judge will end up in Hell, because they have displeased Allah and angered Him by not dealing with people in fairness. Penalties must always be fair and balanced to reflect the crime. When leniency is required, judges should be lenient and when harshness is required then that must be shown, but all of it must be done in a fair manner.

The third judge is a person who is incompetent and ignorant but fancies themself as a knowledgeable person and thinks they are capable of judging between people. They are ignorant; therefore, they have no right to take up this post in the first place and consequently, they will be punished in Hell.

This hadith teaches us that positions of power and authority should only be taken up by people of competency and capacity. If a position is offered and you are not worthy of that post, you should decline and not let the temptation of power get to you. An incompetent person may do more harm than good. The damage caused could be devastating to the lives of many people, whereby undoing the wrong and setting things right might not be an option. In many instances, poor judgement may lead to severe consequences and it may not be possible to reverse things.

What Breaks a Fast?

عَنْ أَبِي هُرَيْرَةَ ﷺ قَالَ قَالَ رَسُولُ اللَّهِ ﷺ مَنْ ذَرَعَهُ قَيْءٌ وَهُوَ
صَائِمٌ فَلَيْسَ عَلَيْهِ قَضَاءٌ وَإِنِ اسْتَقَاءَ فَلْيَقْضِ

Abū Hurayrah ﷺ narrated that the Messenger of Allah ﷺ said: 'If one has a sudden attack of vomiting while he is fasting, no atonement is required of him; but if he vomits intentionally, he must make atonement.'

Fasting is a special type of worship. What makes it special is its covert nature in that no one can know who is fasting and who is not. Unlike other acts of worship, fasting takes up the entire daytime and lasts for several hours. The sacrifice of food and water causes hardship and discomfort for us, yet we do it only for the sake of Allah and His pleasure. The special nature of fasting is recognised by Allah and He tells us that He alone will reward the person for their fasts.[4] In other words, the reward of fasting does not conform to the conventional way of rewarding actions from 70 to 700 units of reward; rather, Allah will personally decide how much reward should be given to the person fasting.

Fasting is a ritual act of worship and is regulated by rules and conditions. Thus, there are certain actions which can violate the principles of fasting and render the fast null and void. In this hadith, the Prophet Muhammad ﷺ wanted to teach Muslims about vomiting and whether or not that breaks a fast. Giving up food and water can affect different people in different ways. Sometimes the absence of food and water can make a person feel sick. Vomiting is the body's way of expelling toxins and foreign substances from the body so as to help the person get better.

The urge to vomit can be natural in the sense that the body forcefully ejects the contents of the stomach. A person has no way of controlling this. In this case, the Prophet Muhammad ﷺ taught us that if this happens to a fasting person, he or she may continue to fast if they feel well enough to do so. However, sometimes a person may feel queasy and feel the *urge* to be sick. If that person decides to make himself or herself sick by inserting their fingers down their throat and thus induce vomiting, they have violated their fast and now must make up for it after the month of Ramadan has ended.

The reason why naturally induced vomiting does not break the fast is because it was out of the control of the person and therefore, they cannot be blamed. However, a person who made themselves sick on purpose is at fault and the blame rests upon them.

〰️

---

4   Al-Bukhari, Sahih al-Bukhari, Hadith no. 5927

11

How Much Water Do You Need to Bathe and Make Ablution?

عَنْ عَائِشَةَ ﷺ أَنَّ النَّبِيَّ ﷺ كَانَ يَغْتَسِلُ بِالصَّاعِ وَيَتَوَضَّأُ بِالْمُدِّ

'Ā'ishah ﷺ narrated that the Prophet ﷺ used to bathe himself with a *sā'* (of water) and perform ablution with a *mudd* (of water).

B eing clean and maintaining personal hygiene are of paramount importance for our personal relationship with Allah as well as with people. Islam has spoken so much about cleanliness and purification on many occasions. So, it is not surprising that the foundation of our ritual acts of worshipping Allah also involves purification and being clean. With regards to *ṣalāh*, it is a condition that a person's clothes, place of prayer and body must be clean in order for the prayer to be valid and accepted. Allah says in the Qur'an: *'Indeed Allah loves those who repent and loves those who keep themselves pure'* (al-Baqarah 2: 222).

Islamic teachings have placed much emphasis on being environmentally conscious and has warned extensively against wastefulness. This hadith teaches us that the Prophet Muhammad ﷺ would make ablution with only one *mudd* of water which is equivalent to about 500 ml; and for bathing, he would use only a *sā'* of water, which is equivalent to about 2 litres. The Prophet Muhammad ﷺ used that amount of water because it was sufficient for him to attain purification; a bigger person may need to use more. The reason why the Prophet ﷺ used this amount of water wasn't because water was scarce in Makkah and Madinah; rather, it was to avoid wastage and the unnecessary use of natural resources. In another hadith, the Prophet ﷺ told his Companions not to use an excessive amount of water when making ablution. One of the Companions had asked him, 'Can there be waste in [5]ablution?' The Prophet ﷺ replied that even if he were by a river, he should not use more water than what he needs.

Looking after the environment is a collective responsibility and avoiding wastage is a moral obligation. Sadly though, our attitude towards dealing with water is one of taking it for granted and we do not think twice when it comes to using water. When washing the dishes, we let the tap run on full-flow and at a stretch. When in the shower, we prolong standing under the water not because we need to clean ourselves but because it feels refreshing and comfortable. When making ablution, the tap runs without a break, and no regard is paid to the water going down the drain.

This hadith teaches us an important lesson on wastage even if there is an abundance of the resource. We should be mindful of turning off the electrical appliances not in use, of switching off the lights when we aren't in the room, of avoiding heating or cooling rooms unnecessarily, and the like. Many people are careless at work because they are not responsible for paying the bills. So the light is left on; or the heating is turned on and when the room gets too hot, rather than turning off the heaters, the windows are opened. The same could also be true of people in hotter countries and air conditioners. However, this should not be

---

5   Ibn Majah, *Sunan Ibn Majah*, Hadith no. 419

the attitude of a Muslim. Any form of wastage is unlawful and anyone who wastes will be answerable to Allah on the Day of Judgement. It is our moral responsibility to look after the Earth, as it was given to us as an *amānah*, a trust.

෴

12

Spiritual Protection from Sudden Illness or Strokes

حَدَّثَنَا أَبُو مَوْدُودٍ عَمَّنْ سَمِعَ أَبَانَ بْنَ عُثْمَانَ ۞ يَقُولُ سَمِعْتُ
عُثْمَانَ ﵁ يَعْنِي ابْنَ عَفَّانَ ﵁ يَقُولُ سَمِعْتُ رَسُولَ اللَّهِ ﷺ
يَقُولُ مَنْ قَالَ بِسْمِ اللَّهِ الَّذِي لاَ يَضُرُّ مَعَ اسْمِهِ شَيْءٌ فِي الْأَرْضِ
وَلاَ فِي السَّمَاءِ وَهُوَ السَّمِيعُ الْعَلِيمُ ثَلَاثَ مَرَّاتٍ لَمْ تُصِبْهُ فَجْأَةُ
بَلَاءٍ حَتَّى يُصْبِحَ وَمَنْ قَالَهَا حِينَ يُصْبِحُ ثَلَاثَ مَرَّاتٍ لَمْ تُصِبْهُ
فَجْأَةُ بَلَاءٍ حَتَّى يُمْسِيَ قَالَ فَأَصَابَ أَبَانَ بْنَ عُثْمَانَ الْفَالِجُ
فَجَعَلَ الرَّجُلُ الَّذِي سَمِعَ مِنْهُ الْحَدِيثَ يَنْظُرُ إِلَيْهِ فَقَالَ لَهُ مَا لَكَ
تَنْظُرُ إِلَيَّ فَوَاللَّهِ مَا كَذَبْتُ عَلَى عُثْمَانَ وَلاَ كَذَبَ عُثْمَانُ عَلَى
النَّبِيِّ صلى الله عليه وسلم وَلَكِنَّ الْيَوْمَ الَّذِي أَصَابَنِي فِيهِ مَا
أَصَابَنِي غَضِبْتُ فَنَسِيتُ أَنْ أَقُولَهَا

Abān ibn ʿUthmān said: 'I heard Uthman ibn ʿAffān ﷺ
say: "I heard the Messenger of Allah ﷺ say: 'If anyone says
three times: "In the Name of Allah, when whose Name
is mentioned nothing on Earth or in Heaven can cause
harm, and He is the Hearer, the Knower," he will not
suffer sudden affliction till the morning, and if anyone says
this in the morning, he will not suffer sudden affliction till
the evening.'"' Abān was afflicted by some paralysis and
when a man who heard the hadith began to look at him,
he said to him: 'Why are you looking at me? I swear by
Allah, I did not tell a lie about Uthman, nor did Uthman
tell a lie about the Prophet ﷺ, but that day when I was
afflicted by it, I became angry and forgot to say them.'

Having dependence on Allah is a very important part of the
Islamic faith. On many occasions Allah commands Muslims
to depend on Him, but this dependence comes after we have done
everything we need to do. For example, if a person buys a car, then
it is up to them to make sure that they look after the car in terms of
regularly servicing it, checking its tyres, keeping it clean and the like.
It is after a person has fulfilled their responsibility, that they should
turn to Allah and hope for the best. If a person takes no responsibility
to look after their car, but simply says 'I will depend on Allah to look
after my car,' then they have failed to understand what depending on
Allah really means.

Another aspect of our lives in which we must take responsibility is
our health. Our health is very important to us and we should take all
precautions to look after it, making sure we exercise regularly, eat well

and sleep well. However, regardless of how well we look after ourselves, it is important to have great dependence on Allah to look after us, because we do not know what truly is happening within our bodies.

This hadith teaches us several important lessons. Firstly, it teaches us a supplication the Messenger of Allah ﷺ taught his followers to recite three times in the morning and three times in the evening, so that they will be protected from sudden illnesses like strokes. Uthman ibn 'Affān, the son-in-law of the Prophet Muhammad ﷺ and the third Caliph of Islam, taught this supplication to his son Abān, who would, every day, recite the supplication: *Bismillāh-hil-ladhī lā yaḍurru ma' ismi-hi shay'un fil arḍi wa lā fi-samā'i wa huwa al-Samī' al-'Alīm.* He practised this supplication and enjoyed good health.

Secondly, Abān taught other people to recite this supplication and they also practised it. Once, Abān was afflicted with some form of paralysis. When people came to visit him, one man looked at him in a strange and curious way as if he doubted the hadith he narrated from his father, Uthman, who narrated it from the Prophet ﷺ—because if indeed the Prophet ﷺ said it, then it was true, in which case, how could Abān be afflicted with paralysis, as he would have been undoubtedly foremost in reciting the supplication? Abān sensed his scepticism and told the man that neither did he lie about his father, Uthman ﷺ nor did Uthman ﷺ make it up. Abān further informed the man that he had forgotten to recite the supplication one day, which was what resulted in his affliction.

Thirdly, anyone can be afflicted with illness. If the great scholar Abān, the son of Uthman ﷺ, can be afflicted with paralysis, then anyone else can be too. These are tests from Allah to see how we respond—do we respond with patience or despair? Abān did not respond with despair, rather he looked at himself and realised his mistake of forgetting to recite the supplication, and was patient with what Allah gave him.

Most of all, the greatest lesson this hadith teaches us is to have dependence on Allah, which goes hand-in-hand with taking the measures to look after ourselves. And one of the ways to look after ourselves is to recite this supplication, which is easy to learn and just as easy to practise.

13

Remembering Allah while Distressed at Night

عَنْ مُعَاذِ بْنِ جَبَلٍ عَنِ النَّبِيِّ ﷺ قَالَ مَا مِنْ مُسْلِمٍ يَبِيتُ عَلَى
ذِكْرٍ طَاهِرًا فَيَتَعَارَّ مِنَ اللَّيْلِ فَيَسْأَلُ اللَّهَ خَيْرًا مِنَ الدُّنْيَا وَالآخِرَةِ
إِلاَّ أَعْطَاهُ إِيَّاهُ

Muʿādh ibn Jabal ◉ narrated that the Prophet ◉ said:
'If a Muslim sleeps while remembering Allah in the state
of purification, then is alarmed while asleep at night and
asks Allah for good in this world and in the Hereafter, He
surely will give it to him.'

Human life is seldom free from stress, worry and toil. It is the way
Allah has designed life to be. Perhaps it is a way for us to know
what good times are and what bad times are, but stress and worry are
most certainly tests from Allah. It does not matter who you are, there
will always be bad times in your life. Perhaps one reason for that is that
when we receive good times again, we will be more grateful to Allah

than we would ever be if we hadn't experienced the bad times in the first place.

Allah has created sleep to help us recuperate and regain our strength. It is one of the most essential parts of our lives and Allah has created the body in such a way that if a person deprives the body of sleep, it will overcome them and the body will forcibly shut down in order to regain its strength. Sometimes what we do during the day can still play on our minds especially if it is an event which is stressful and worrying. During sleep the mind is still active and if we feel distressed it can wake us up with troubled thoughts. The Prophet Muhammad ﷺ told us that if a person goes to sleep at night in a state of purification while mentioning Allah before he sleeps, and is awakened due to distress and at that moment, he asks Allah for any of the goodness of this world and the next, then Allah will surely grant him it.

This is truly an amazing hadith and it teaches us that even at times of worry and distress Allah has provided us a means of salvation and help. This requires composure, and may sound easier than it truly is. Consider what Thābit al-Bunānī, a great *tabi'ī* (successor), narrated in this regard. He said: 'Abū Ẓabyah came to visit us, and he transmitted this hadith to us from Mu'ādh ibn Jabal ﷺ from the Prophet ﷺ' and added that a person came to him and told him that he tried his best to utter these (prayers) when he got up but could not do so. The hadith commentator, al-Mubārakpūrī, says that may be because he kept on forgetting or due to some other reason. This shows that it requires great effort and attentiveness for us to recall this hadith and put it into practise when awoken in the middle of sleep.

However, just because that person could not do it, it does not mean that you cannot. A person should seize every opportunity to be mindful of Allah and try their best to ask Allah for help and to grant them their wishes. This hadith teaches us that Allah loves us and gives us many opportunities to ask Him for His help. It is our duty to grab on to these chances and win His favours.

14

What is Better Than Ṣadaqah?

عَنْ أَبِى الدَّرْدَاءِ ﴾ قَالَ قَالَ رَسُولُ اللهِ ﴾ أَلاَ أُخْبِرُكُمْ بِأَفْضَلَ مِنْ دَرَجَةِ الصِّيَامِ وَالصَّلاَةِ وَالصَّدَقَةِ قَالُوا بَلَى قَالَ إِصْلاَحُ ذَاتِ الْبَيْنِ وَفَسَادُ ذَاتِ الْبَيْنِ الْحَالِقَةُ

Abū al-Dardā' ﴾ narrated the Prophet ﴾ said: 'Shall I not inform you of something more excellent in degree than fasting, prayer and almsgiving (*ṣadaqah*)?' The people replied: 'Yes, Prophet of Allah!' He said: 'It is putting things right between people; while spoiling them is the shaver (destructive).'

This hadith is amazing in terms of the lesson it gives us. Let us elaborate on it so we can understand the hadith in context. The reason Allah created us was to worship Him. There is no secondary reason or purpose for human existence, and our aim and objective should be to worship Allah alone. In order to teach us how to worship Him, Allah has sent His Messenger Muhammad ﷺ. There are some major acts of worship such as prayer, fasting, hajj and zakat which represent the religion of Islam as ways of worshipping Allah. Nobody can deny these aspects of Islam without denying Islam itself; this is how important prayer, fasting, hajj and zakat are to Islam. The Qur'an and Hadith are a testament to the high significance of these acts of worship, and because they represent the religion of Islam there cannot be any action more significant than them.

Prayer is the direct connection we have with Allah. A person communicates with Allah during prayer and Allah responds to His servant who is worshipping Him. Nothing brings us closer to Allah and nothing removes sin as quickly as prayer. Fasting is an act of great sacrifice, where we give up food and drink for many hours for the sake of Allah, to seek His pleasure and get our prayers answered. Fasting is so special to Allah that He makes a point of personally rewarding the person fasting. The act of *ṣadaqah* or charity is much emphasised in the Qur'an to the extent that it is mentioned in the opening lines of many chapters of the Qur'an. The perpetual reward of charity is extolled in the Qur'an and ahadith.

Despite the undeniably special status of prayer, fasting and *ṣadaqah*, this hadith tells us that the Prophet Muhammad ﷺ wanted to teach us that there is something better than all three of those acts. Putting things right between people is more virtuous and pious. Conversely, the evil of creating rift between people comes with severe punishment. This is because there is no point of praying, fasting and giving hundreds and thousands or even millions in charity, and at the same time creating discord and animosity between people.

This hadith in effect places the importance of social harmony and communityship above and beyond the sanctity of ritual acts of worshipping Allah. It is a duty upon everyone to mediate between people who have fallen out, create friendship and build relationships.

All good acts of worship mean little if there is no peace and amicable bonds between people in society. Everyone must know that all Muslims are declared by Allah as brothers and sisters regardless of skin colour, culture or ethnicity.

Details of the Day of Judgement

عَنْ حُذَيْفَةَ ﷺ قَالَ قَامَ فِينَا رَسُولُ اللهِ ﷺ قَائِمًا فَمَا تَرَكَ شَيْئًا يَكُونُ فِي مَقَامِهِ ذَلِكَ إِلَى قِيَامِ السَّاعَةِ إِلاَّ حَدَّثَهُ حَفِظَهُ مَنْ حَفِظَهُ وَنَسِيَهُ مَنْ نَسِيَهُ قَدْ عَلِمَهُ أَصْحَابُهُ هَؤُلاَءِ وَإِنَّهُ لَيَكُونُ مِنْهُ الشَّيْءُ فَأَذْكُرُهُ كَمَا يَذْكُرُ الرَّجُلُ وَجْهَ الرَّجُلِ إِذَا غَابَ عَنْهُ ثُمَّ إِذَا رَآهُ عَرَفَهُ

Hudhayfah ﷺ narrated: 'The Messenger of Allah ﷺ stood among us (to address us) and he left out nothing that would happen up to the last hour without telling of it. Some remembered it and some forgot, and these Companions of his have known it. When something of it which I have forgotten happens, I remembered it, just as a man remembers another's face when he is away and recognises him when he sees him.'

This world is finite, and it will come to an end. This fact is not denied by anyone regardless of their faith. The message that this world will come to an end was taught by every prophet to their communities. The reason for this is to confirm to them that the Hereafter is close and what they do with their life on Earth is important to determine their place in the Hereafter.

The significance of the Day of Judgement with respect to the Prophet Muhammad ﷺ is that his prophethood signalled the first of the major signs of the Day of Judgement. The Prophet ﷺ wanted to teach his followers what to look out for as indicators that the Final Hour is drawing closer.

This hadith teaches us that Allah told His Prophet ﷺ all the relevant events related to the Day of Judgement, and in turn the Prophet ﷺ informed us of them. The long list of events meant that not everyone could remember them in sequence like the Prophet ﷺ told them, but the narrator of the hadith, Hudhayfah ؓ, said that although he wasn't able to remember all of them in sequence, if he were to encounter any of them, he would recognise it instantly.

The signs of the Day of Judgement can be divided into two groups: major signs and minor signs. Many scholars have said that most of the minor signs have already appeared. The hardship during the appearance of the major signs will be great and very difficult, and it will require strong faith to pass through them. Confusion, doubt, chaos and lies will be the order of the day. The Prophet ﷺ told us of the signs of the Day of Judgement to guard ourselves against its evil and taught us to seek the protection of Allah from it, in particular the trials of the anti-Christ, Dajjāl.

The Virtues of Reading the Qur'an

عَنْ أَنَسٍ ﷺ قَالَ قَالَ رَسُولُ اللهِ ﷺ مَثَلُ الْمُؤْمِنِ الَّذِى يَقْرَأُ
الْقُرْآنَ مَثَلُ الأُتْرُجَّةِ رِيحُهَا طَيِّبٌ وَطَعْمُهَا طَيِّبٌ وَمَثَلُ الْمُؤْمِنِ
الَّذِى لاَ يَقْرَأُ الْقُرْآنَ كَمَثَلِ التَّمَرَةِ طَعْمُهَا طَيِّبٌ وَلاَ رِيحَ لَهَا وَمَثَلُ
الْفَاجِرِ الَّذِى يَقْرَأُ الْقُرْآنَ كَمَثَلِ الرَّيْحَانَةِ رِيحُهَا طَيِّبٌ وَطَعْمُهَا
مُرٌّ وَمَثَلُ الْفَاجِرِ الَّذِى لاَ يَقْرَأُ الْقُرْآنَ كَمَثَلِ الْحَنْظَلَةِ طَعْمُهَا مُرٌّ
وَلاَ رِيحَ لَهَا وَمَثَلُ الْجَلِيسِ الصَّالِحِ كَمَثَلِ صَاحِبِ الْمِسْكِ إِنْ لَمْ
يُصِبْكَ مِنْهُ شَىْءٌ أَصَابَكَ مِنْ رِيحِهِ وَمَثَلُ جَلِيسِ السُّوءِ كَمَثَلِ
صَاحِبِ الْكِيرِ إِنْ لَمْ يُصِبْكَ مِنْ سَوَادِهِ أَصَابَكَ مِنْ دُخَانِهِ

Anas ibn Mālik ﷺ narrated the Prophet ﷺ said: 'A
believer who recites the Qur'an is like a citron whose
fragrance is sweet and whose taste is sweet; a believer

who does not recite the Qur'an is like a date which has no fragrance but has sweet taste; a corrupt Muslim who recites the Qur'an is like basil whose fragrance is sweet but whose taste is bitter; and the corrupt Muslim who does not recite the Qur'an is like the colocynth which has a bitter taste and has no fragrance. A good companion is like a man who has musk; if nothing of it reaches you, its fragrance will (certainly) reach you; and a bad companion is like a man who has bellows; if its (black) soot does not reach you, its smoke will (certainly) reach you.'

Let us ask ourselves: How many times do we read the Qur'an in a week? If the answer is 'not many' then we really need to make reciting the Qur'an a daily 'must do' act of worship. The recitation of the Qur'an is voluntary and there is much benefit for the reciter of the Qur'an. In this hadith, the Prophet Muhammad ﷺ described to us the quality of different people who read or do not read the Qur'an.

First, the Prophet ﷺ describes a person who is a proper believer, observes the laws of Allah and abstains from what is forbidden. The Prophet ﷺ describes such a believer as a citron which is a citrus fruit with a thick rind, much like a lemon. It is large, fragrant and delicious to eat with food. Likewise, the recitation of the Qur'an brings out the sweetness and the fragrance of the believer through his or her behaviour, character and conduct with others.

The second person the Prophet ﷺ describes is a believer who has good character, but does not recite the Qur'an. Although such a believer avoids the unlawful and enjoins what is good, he or she lacks the goodness that comes from a believer who recites the Qur'an. A good believer who practises his or her faith but does not read the

Qur'an is like a date fruit. The Prophet ﷺ said it is sweet which reflects the good character of the person, but the date fruit has no aroma. There is nothing wrong with the date, but it is incomplete as a perfect and ideal fruit.

There are some corrupt Muslims who also recite the Qur'an. A corrupt Muslim is the one who commits sin regularly and does not repent or try to stop it. Although they may be corrupt, they might have the good habit of reading the Qur'an. The Prophet ﷺ likened such a person to basil whose fragrance is sweet but taste is bitter. In other words, the act of reciting the Qur'an is wonderful and beautifies a person externally but reading the words of God has not yielded any results in terms of changing their character. Such a person must stop whatever sin they are committing and act upon what they are reciting.

Finally, the Prophet ﷺ describes a person who is corrupt and does not recite the Qur'an as a colocynth. A colocynth is a very unpleasant tasting fruit, it is bitter and devoid of any good smell. A corrupt Muslim who doesn't even recite the Qur'an is exactly that, unpleasant and of little use.

It is interesting to note here that the Prophet ﷺ is giving fruits as an example to explain what he is saying. The reason for this is that eating is a regular activity which everyone can relate to, and it is also a multi-sensory experience. The two most important factors in enjoying food are taste and smell. If either is lacking in the food, it won't give us full enjoyment.

So, how does one become a better person? Humans are social creatures and Allah has created us to be in need of other people to survive. We like to imitate others and that is why companies spend millions on getting famous people to advertise their products. For a person who seeks to be better and do good deeds, they should seek the companionship of those who are pious. This is what the Prophet ﷺ was saying in the second part of the hadith. If you are surrounded by the influence of good people, it will rub off on you. If you are surrounded by those who swear, use insulting words, drink and abuse drugs or engage in any other bad actions then sooner or later that will have an effect on you. In like manner, if you surround yourself with the pious and God-fearing, those who pray without fail and those who engage in good deeds such as reading the Qur'an and giving charity, the influence of those people will rub off on you.

In this hadith, the Prophet Muhammad ﷺ has described four types of people in terms of their relationship with the Qur'an. It is important that you ask yourself which category you fall into.

The Virtues of Sitting at the Place of Prayer

عَنْ أَبِي هُرَيْرَةَ ﷺ أَنَّ رَسُولَ اللَّهِ ﷺ قَالَ الْمَلَائِكَةُ تُصَلِّي عَلَى أَحَدِكُمْ مَا دَامَ فِي مُصَلَّاهُ الَّذِى صَلَّى فِيهِ مَا لَمْ يُحْدِثْ أَوْ يَقُمِ اللَّهُمَّ اغْفِرْ لَهُ اللَّهُمَّ ارْحَمْهُ

Abū Hurayrah ﷺ reported the Messenger of Allah ﷺ
as saying: 'The angels invoke blessings, saying: "O Allah,
forgive him; O Allah, have mercy on him," on any of you
who remains sitting at the place where he offered his prayers
so long as he has not broken his ablution or stands up.'

Everyone needs some time to reflect and contemplate. This is an important part of self-development and personal growth. Our lives can become rapidly busy and occupied with worldly affairs. Despite how busy our lives get it is important for us to take some time out and spend it in reflection.

In this hadith, the Prophet Muhammad ﷺ teaches us the virtues of remaining seated after the prayer, and by doing so he encourages us to engage in the remembrance of Allah (*dhikr*). Once we leave the place of prayer, we become once again engaged with worldly affairs. In order to minimise this, the Prophet ﷺ teaches us to remain seated for as long as possible even if we do not say anything or do anything. To do so comes with great reward. We are informed that the angels of Allah pray for us when we do so, asking Allah to show us mercy and grant us forgiveness, provided we remain with ablution (*wuḍū'*) and do not get up to leave. The fact that angels ask Allah to forgive and show mercy to a person who remains seated after prayer shows the high status of such action as it also reflects the honour of such a person.

The common excuse people have is, 'we are very busy' or 'we don't have time'. It is important to learn to make time for reflection, and the good news is that it becomes easier to do so once it becomes a habit. We will always get busy and occupied with things, but it is about making time, having discipline and setting priorities. Allah has given us the opportunity to achieve rewards very easily and with minimal effort. The question is, do we take advantage of these opportunities?

18

Getting our Prayers Answered

عَنْ أَنَسِ بْنِ مَالِكٍ ﷺ قَالَ قَالَ رَسُولُ اللَّهِ ﷺ لاَ يُرَدُّ الدُّعَاءُ بَيْنَ الأَذَانِ وَالإِقَامَةِ

Anas ibn Mālik ﷺ narrates that the Messenger of Allah ﷺ said: 'The supplication made between the *adhān* and the *iqāmah* is not rejected.'

It is important to understand the difference between Allah granting someone's prayer and Allah rejecting the prayer. Not granting the prayer does not mean that Allah has rejected it. Allah always responds to all good prayers. If the prayer is not granted in this life, then our patience for it will be rewarded in the Hereafter. Our role is to have a strong relationship with Allah, no matter what.

Human life is always in need of something and we always pray to Allah to accept our wishes. Having dependency on Allah is a very important and beautiful part of Islamic belief and practice. One of the key relationships a person should have with Allah is certainty that when one calls upon Allah, Allah hears the call and responds back to it. Allah extolls us to pray to Him and ask Him for what we need.

Once, a man came to the Prophet ﷺ and asked him, 'Is Allah close so we should ask him quietly or is He far from us so we need to raise our voice when we ask him?' Allah answers this question in the Qur'an: *'And when My servant asks you about[6] me, (tell him) I am indeed close. I (listen and) respond to the prayer of every suppliant made to me. So let them (listen and) respond to My call (for obedience to Me) and believe in Me, that they may walk in the right path'* (al-Baqarah 2: 186). In another verse, Allah commands us to pray to Him and He will answer our prayers: *'Call me and I will respond to you'* (Ghāfir 40: 60).

Allah is the Most Merciful and Most Kind and as such He has made ample opportunities of special times during the year, month, day and hour to answer our prayers. One such time is after the *adhān* for prayer has been called till the call that congregational prayer will start, known as the *iqāmah*, is called. This event takes place daily, and for Muslims living in places where the *adhān* is called out loudly, it is impossible to miss it. These are opportunities for Muslims to stop and engage in praying to Allah, asking Him for what they want and what they need. When the Prophet Muhammad ﷺ has reassured us that the supplications we make between the *adhān* and the *iqāmah* are not rejected, that is a serious opportunity for us to have our prayers answered; the rest is up to us to seize them and make the best of the occasion.

It should be noted that Allah may not grant us what we want immediately; sometimes it takes many years before it happens, and sometimes Allah just does not give us what we have been praying for in this world. Some may wonder, 'What's the point of prayer if Allah does not answer the prayer?' The answer to that is that Allah has not made life on Earth to be exactly the way we want everything to be. A

---

6   Al-Qurtubi, *Al-Jami' li-Ahkam al-Qur'an*, Vol. 1, p. 236

responsible father will not give his child everything he or she wants even though he can afford to do it. There may be many reasons for that, one of which might be that it might not be in the best interest of that child to receive what he or she asked for. In like manner, Allah knows best, and He will give us what He knows is in our best interest. As for us, we are commanded to ask Allah for what we need; whether our prayer is accepted or not is in the Hands of Allah, but our reward for asking Allah is guaranteed.

༺ঔ৩

19

The Good Deeds of a Child

عَنِ ابْنِ عَبَّاسٍ ﷺ قَالَ كَانَ رَسُولُ اللهِ ﷺ بِالرَّوْحَاءِ فَلَقِيَ رَكْبًا فَسَلَّمَ عَلَيْهِمْ فَقَالَ مَنِ الْقَوْمُ فَقَالُوا الْمُسْلِمُونَ فَقَالُوا فَمَنْ أَنْتُمْ قَالُوا رَسُولُ اللهِ ﷺ فَفَزِعَتِ امْرَأَةٌ فَأَخَذَتْ بِعَضُدِ صَبِيٍّ فَأَخْرَجَتْهُ مِنْ مِحَفَّتِهَا فَقَالَتْ يَا رَسُولَ اللهِ هَلْ لِهَذَا حَجٌّ قَالَ نَعَمْ وَلَكِ أَجْرٌ

Ibn 'Abbās ﷺ said the Messenger of Allah ﷺ was at *al-Rawḥā'*. There he met some riders. He saluted them and asked who they were. They replied that they were Muslims. They asked, 'Who you are?' They (the Companions) replied he is the Messenger of Allah ﷺ. A woman became anxious, taking her child by his arm and lifting him from her litter on the camel. She said: 'O Messenger of Allah, is it valid for this (child) to perform hajj?' He replied: 'Yes, and you will have a reward.'

This hadith records an encounter the Prophet Muhammad ﷺ had with a group of people who were on a journey to perform the pilgrimage. They did not know each other and so the Prophet Muhammad ﷺ greeted them with the *salām* first and asked them to introduce themselves. They replied that they were Muslims, but they did not recognise the Messenger of Islam. The Prophet's Companions replied that this is the Messenger of Allah ﷺ. A woman became anxious to clarify something from the Prophet ﷺ, so she took her child from the carriage and showed him to the Prophet ﷺ. The Prophet ﷺ not only told her that what she did was valid, but that she will also enjoy the reward of the child's good deeds.

In Islam, children remain innocent and no part of the law applies to them until they reach puberty. Children are born innocent and they have no sense of what is good and what is bad, and therefore they need good direction from their guardians to teach them what is right and what is wrong, what is lawful and what is unlawful. Consider a child that is bought up in a household where bad language is used frequently; what is the likelihood of such a child growing up using bad language? Such a child will not think that there is a problem in using offensive language. Conversely, if a child is bought up in a household where no bad language is used, then it is highly likely that the child will not use bad language. The way children are raised is important because they are our future, they are a gift from Allah, and so we have a responsibility to teach them good values, morals and ethics.

There are two things this hadith teaches us. Firstly, that we will ultimately benefit in both worlds if we bring up our children with good manners, a strong religious identity and religious practises. Secondly, the pilgrimage a child may perform does not count as their actual hajj which is due only after puberty. This is the view of the majority of the scholars of Islam. The Prophet's response in the affirmative was to express his approval for her bringing her child to the hajj. The child will be rewarded and the parents will get their share of reward too, but hajj is still an obligation that must be performed by the child after puberty at least once in their life. The same applies to all other obligatory acts of worship such as prayer, fasting, *'umrah*, charity and the like.

❦

20

The Prophet's Qurbānī (Uḍḥiyah)

عَنْ عَائِشَةَ ﷺ أَنَّ رَسُولَ اللَّهِ ﷺ أَمَرَ بِكَبْشٍ أَقْرَنَ يَطَأُ فِي سَوَادٍ وَيَنْظُرُ فِي سَوَادٍ وَيَبْرُكُ فِي سَوَادٍ فَأُتِيَ بِهِ فَضَحَّى بِهِ فَقَالَ يَا عَائِشَةُ هَلُمِّي الْمُدْيَةَ ثُمَّ قَالَ اشْحَذِيهَا بِحَجَرٍ فَفَعَلَتْ فَأَخَذَهَا وَأَخَذَ الْكَبْشَ فَأَضْجَعَهُ وَذَبَحَهُ وَقَالَ بِسْمِ اللَّهِ اللَّهُمَّ تَقَبَّلْ مِنْ مُحَمَّدٍ وَآلِ مُحَمَّدٍ وَمِنْ أُمَّةِ مُحَمَّدٍ ثُمَّ ضَحَّى بِهِ صلى الله عليه وسلم

Narrated 'Ā'ishah ﷺ: 'The Messenger of Allah ﷺ ordered a horned ram with black legs, black belly and black round the eyes, and it was brought for him to sacrifice. He said: "'Ā'ishah, get the knife," then he said, "sharpen it with a stone." So, I did. He took the knife and then took the ram and placed it on the ground in preparation of its sacrifice. He then said: "In the Name of Allah. O Allah, accept it for Muhammad, Muhammad's family and the followers of Muhammad." Then he slaughtered it.'

Sacrifice is the cornerstone of worship. All acts of worship require sacrifice and a level of hardship. For example, prayer requires ablution, movement, stopping work or getting up from sleep. Observing all of this can cause inconvenience. But that is the meaning of worship. We make small sacrifices because we love Allah and are grateful for everything that He has given us, and the way we show our gratitude is by worshipping Him. Fasting, hajj and zakat also require sacrifice of different levels. In summary, worshipping Allah cannot be conceived without there being a degree of sacrifice.

There is one act of worship which requires a literal sacrifice. This is known as *uḍḥiyah* or *qurbāni* in many parts of the Muslim world. This tradition started from the Prophet Ibrāhīm 🙶 who was commanded by Allah to show his commitment to Allah by sacrificing his beloved son Ismā'īl 🙶. This was a test from Allah and when Prophet Ibrāhīm 🙶 was about to sacrifice his son, Allah stopped him and replaced his son with a ram. It is this act of sacrifice that Muslims are commanded to imitate in the hope of learning what real sacrifice means. Allah has commanded all Muslims who can afford to buy an animal for sacrifice to perform this great act of worship. The meat should be divided into three parts: one for the person and their family, another portion for the poor and another portion for friends and relatives.

This hadith teaches us a number of things. Firstly, animal welfare is an important part of this ritual and all care must be taken to look after the animal and cause it the least distress possible. Proper tools for the job are essential so that the animal feels minimal pain. Secondly, the animal was made to rest on its side. Al-Nawawī explains that *idja'* is to lie the animal on its left-hand side because it causes the animal less stress. Thirdly, this hadith teaches us that it is praiseworthy to have a big mature animal rather than one that is too small. Fourthly, most scholars say that one animal is enough for an entire family, but some scholars say that if other members of the family can afford it then they should make another sacrifice individually.

One of the great spiritual lessons we can learn is performing an act of worship on behalf of other people. The Prophet Muhammad ﷺ made a sacrifice saying that it was on behalf of himself, his family and his followers. Many scholars say that it is permissible to make the sacrifice on behalf of other people even if they are deceased. Both the deceased and the person making the sacrifice will be rewarded for the animal sacrificed for Allah's sake.

༺ৡ৹

21

The Prophet Always Offered the Night Prayer (Tahajjud)

قَالَتْ عَائِشَةُ ﷺ لَا تَدَعْ قِيَامَ اللَّيْلِ فَإِنَّ رَسُولَ اللهِ ﷺ كَانَ لَا
يَدَعُهُ وَكَانَ إِذَا مَرِضَ أَوْ كَسِلَ صَلَّى قَاعِدًا

'Ā'ishah ﷺ said: 'Do not give up prayer at night, for the
Messenger of Allah ﷺ would not leave it. If he fell ill or
lethargic, he would offer it sitting.'

Allah says in the Qur'an: *'O you (sleeping and) enwrapped in sheets
(muzzammil). Stand up in prayer by night, all but a small part of it.
Half of it or reduce it a little. Or add to it a little. And recite the Qur'an
slowly and distinctly'* (al-Muzzammil 73: 1–4).

There are certain things which are too valuable and precious to let
go. According to some scholars, Allah initially made the night-
prayer, known as *tahajjud*, obligatory upon the Prophet ﷺ. When the
command came to stand for prayer the entire night, the Prophet ﷺ
and his Companions did so. Eventually, the night prayer continued

to be a voluntary act of worship upon the Muslims but the Prophet Muhammad ﷺ continued to observe this prayer consistently, even during illness or travel.

The *tahajjud* prayer has many special and unique benefits. One of the greatest benefits is the reward of having the special attention of Allah. *Tahajjud* is prayed at a time when most people are fast asleep; so when some believers, in the stupor of sleep, choose to wake up and stand in front of Allah, bowing and prostrating to Him, they become special to Him. This is an immense sacrifice and it comes with great reward, because Allah calls out to people at this time of the night and says, 'Is there anyone calling Me so that I may grant their prayers? Is there anyone asking for forgiveness so that I may forgive him?'[7] This is the best time for a person to gain the favour of Allah and get their wishes answered. Imam Shāfiʿī said: 'The *duʿāʾ* made at *tahajjud* is like an arrow which does not miss its target.'[8] When we forsake our sleep, perform *wuḍūʾ* earnestly, and stand in prayer to Allah in the stillness of the night, we will experience a connection to Him like no other. During that moment of quiet solitude in front of our Lord, we will instinctively open up and pour our heart out to Him in humility and submissiveness.

This hadith records that the Prophet ﷺ always prayed the night prayer. Even if the Prophet ﷺ was feeling tired or ill, he would get up for the *tahajjud* prayer. If he was unable to stand and pray, he would sit and observe the prayer.

Ideally, the *tahajjud* prayer should be offered in the final third of the night, but it can be prayed at any time after the Ishāʾ prayer. It is better to pray it in units of two (*rakaʿah*s) but some scholars say four units are better. It is praiseworthy that the recitation be aloud but not so much as to disturb anyone sleeping. It is extremely praiseworthy

---

7   Al-Bukhari, Al-Adab al-Mufrad, Hadith no. 753

8   Al-Shafiʿi, *Diwan*, p. 17

that the recitation be long, and the bowing and the prostration be also long. A person can choose to offer as many units of prayer as they like. After prayers, a person should not forget to make supplication and should seize the moment to ask Allah for what they want in this life and the next.

22

What to Break Fasts With

عن أَنَسِ بْنَ مَالِكٍ ﷺ قال كَانَ رَسُولُ اللَّهِ ﷺ يُفْطِرُ عَلَى رُطَبَاتٍ
قَبْلَ أَنْ يُصَلِّيَ فَإِنْ لَمْ تَكُنْ رُطَبَاتٌ فَعَلَى تَمَرَاتٍ فَإِنْ لَمْ تَكُنْ
حَسَا حَسَوَاتٍ مِنْ مَاءٍ

Anas ibn Mālik ﷺ narrates: 'The Messenger of Allah ﷺ
used to break his fast before praying with some fresh dates;
but if there were no fresh dates, he had a few dry dates,
and if there were no dry dates, he took some sips of water.'

Fasting is one of the great acts of worshipping Allah and it is one the
five pillars of Islam. Allah created human beings in a way that they
would desire food. Although we need food to survive, eating for us is
more than just survival. It is a pleasurable experience, a social event and
one that most humans anticipate. Food is one of the greatest ways we
show our love to people, how much we honour them and how much
they mean to us. Therefore, when a person gives up food intentionally

for no other reason except for the love of Allah and seeking His pleasure, this reflects the deep connection a person has with Allah.

During the month of Ramadan when Muslims fast, they prepare different dishes to eat. This hadith teaches us two main things. Firstly, when it came to the time to break the fast, the Prophet Muhammad ﷺ broke his fast with dates. His preference was fresh dates. If fresh dates were unavailable, the Prophet ﷺ would eat dry dates instead. One of the reasons why the Prophet ﷺ would prefer fresh dates over dried dates was to highlight the virtue of fresh food. The nutriments in fresh food are always higher and better than what's found in dried or preserved foodstuff. If dried dates were unavailable, the Prophet ﷺ would break his fast with water. It is good practice to eat something light after depriving the body of food for several hours. Eating something light allows the body to process and digest the food better. There are many benefits of eating dates with some claiming that dates are rich in antioxidants, they help with balancing blood sugar levels and blood pressure as well. Regardless of the health benefits, Muslims should break their fast with dates because the Prophet Muhammad ﷺ broke his fasts with dates.

This hadith also teaches us the simple nature of the Prophet Muhammad ﷺ and his humble provisions. At times, the Prophet ﷺ did not have fresh dates perhaps because they were out of season, but the fact that he did not have dried dates too at those times shows the simplicity of his life. While we have many dishes to eat after fasting and then complain if the food is not tasty enough, the Prophet Muhammad ﷺ never complained that he did not have enough food to eat. Let us take some time to think about the Prophet Muhammad ﷺ, his greatness, his leadership, his prophethood and his status amongst creation. History is a testament that chiefs and leaders always lived a better life than anyone around them, because they would set up systems to benefit them and serve them. The Prophet's life was completely different. Despite being the best of the best, he lived a simple and basic life, serving others and not himself.

❧ 23 ❧

Seeing the Person You Propose to Marry

عَنْ جَابِرِ بْنِ عَبْدِ اللَّهِ ﷺ قَالَ قَالَ رَسُولُ اللَّهِ ﷺ إِذَا خَطَبَ أَحَدُكُمُ الْمَرْأَةَ فَإِنِ اسْتَطَاعَ أَنْ يَنْظُرَ إِلَى مَا يَدْعُوهُ إِلَى نِكَاحِهَا فَلْيَفْعَلْ

Jābir ibn 'Abdullāh ﷺ narrated that the Prophet ﷺ said: 'When one of you seeks a woman in marriage, if he is able to look at her, he should do so.'

Marriage is an important part of human life and Islam. The Prophet Muhammad ﷺ on many occasions condemned celibacy and encouraged his followers to marry. Once a man was bragging about his celibacy and when the Prophet ﷺ heard it, he got angry and told the man off in strong terms. The Prophet ﷺ denounced it as against his Sunnah or his way of life, which is the way of life Muslims are commanded to follow.

Marriage is the lawful institution for establishing a family and fulfilling the natural human sexual desire. Allah has created men and women so that they can establish companionship and provide help and care for each other. To have a person you can rely on gives you a great sense of satisfaction and security. Allah has created human beings with the desire to seek companionship, and there can be no stronger companionship than that between a husband and wife.

Finding a spouse can be a challenging affair. It is important that a person tries to find a partner they are compatible with, someone who shares common values and has similar likes and dislikes. Having physical attraction is also a key ingredient to having a successful marriage. Arranged marriages, that is to say, marriages organised by the guardians were the normal convention of matrimonial affairs. The parents would seek suitable partners for their children. In most cases where the marriage was arranged, the parents would agree to all the terms of the marriage and the couple would not even see each other before the marriage. This custom existed in many cultures and still continues to do so in some parts of the world. However, the tradition is changing, and the common practice now is that prospective couples do see each other.

The Prophet's teaching is clear regarding this. He has encouraged prospective couples to see each other before committing to marriage, because seeing each other will help create chemistry and establish physical attraction. The reason why this is important is because there are strict rules in Islam about male and female interactions. Islam recognises the power of physical attraction between opposite sexes, which is why dating and free mixing is disallowed in the first place, as it could lead to committing sinful acts. At the same time, Islam also recognises that physical attraction remains one of the factors for a strong marital relationship, and so it gives people the chance to determine this with a potential spouse right at the beginning.

Meeting the person one intends to marry, in the presence of the prospective bride's *maḥram*, is a good way of testing if there is attraction, because for many people attraction is the foremost factor in deciding whether or not to further the discussion of marriage. Due to the important nature of physical attraction, the Prophet encouraged people to at least see each other before committing to marriage.

Do Not Overstay
Your Welcome

عَنْ أَبِي شُرَيْحٍ الْكَعْبِيّ ﷺ أَنَّ رَسُولَ اللهِ ﷺ قَالَ مَنْ كَانَ يُؤْمِنُ
بِاللهِ وَالْيَوْمِ الآخِرِ فَلْيُكْرِمْ ضَيْفَهُ جَائِزَتُهُ يَوْمُهُ وَلَيْلَتُهُ الضِّيَافَةُ
ثَلاَثَةُ أَيَّامٍ وَمَا بَعْدَ ذَلِكَ فَهُوَ صَدَقَةٌ وَلاَ يَحِلُّ لَهُ أَنْ يَثْوِىَ عِنْدَهُ
حَتَّى يُحْرِجَهُ

Abū Shurayḥ al-Kaʿbī ﷺ reported the Messenger of Allah
ﷺ as saying: 'He who believes in Allah and the Last Day
should honour his guest by supplying him with provisions
for the road that will serve him for a day and night.
Hospitality extends for three days; anything beyond that is
ṣadaqah (charity); and it is not lawful that a guest should
stay till he makes himself an encumbrance.'

During the time of the Prophet Muhammad ﷺ, travelling was an arduous affair. It was difficult because the roads were not as good as the modern roads we have today. Short travel would require many hours and days, while long-distance travel often took weeks and months. Travelling was extremely stressful and required meticulous planning and management. If food and water were not managed properly it could be a matter of life and death. There were no guest houses, no inns and no service stations, which meant that people would have to camp at night. Food and water were always limited because an animal can only carry so much. Unlike today, travelling was never a luxury experience for people, and therefore travellers often needed help and a place to stay.

The Prophet Muhammad ﷺ was keen to teach his followers the importance of treating guests with hospitality and kindness, making it a part of the Islamic faith. The Prophet ﷺ used strong words in this regard. 'He who believes in Allah and the Last Day' denotes that honouring guests is no trivial matter, but one of belief in Allah and the Final Day. In this hadith, the Prophet Muhammad ﷺ teaches us three important lessons.

Firstly, a good Muslim host will care for their guests by providing them with sufficient provision for one day. Imam Abū Dāwūd said: 'Imam Mālik was asked about the explanation of the Prophet's statement about supplying the guest with provisions for the road that will serve for a day and night. Imam Mālik said it means that a person should honour the guest, present him some gifts and take care of him for a day and night.'

Secondly, the Prophet ﷺ teaches us that a guest has the right to be looked after for up to three days. This is the obligation upon every Muslim towards their guests. If their guests stay beyond three days then they have no obligation to look after them, but they will be rewarded the reward of charity if they continue their hospitality.

The third lesson the Prophet ﷺ teaches us is an ethical lesson, that is to say, not to abuse the generosity of the host. When guests are present in a household, it takes away the freedom and comfort of the host. This temporary loss of freedom is tolerated for the sake of providing the guests with a good staying experience. However, this cannot be sustainable, and it will only be a matter of time before the guests become an annoyance for the host. Guests should be mindful of this, which is why the Prophet Muhammad ﷺ has taught us that it is unlawful for us to outstay our welcome at anyone's house.

This hadith teaches us an important social etiquette of being mindful of looking after guests and being hospitable to them. It also teaches us, as guests, to not cause our hosts inconvenience and embarrass them by forcing them to ask us to leave. This should be the code of conduct in all our daily affairs. When we go to visit someone, we should not stay so long at their house that it causes them annoyance. While this hadith speaks about overstaying at someone's place, we could apply the same etiquette when speaking to someone on the phone, or on the road or at work or the like. It would be good to read the room in such instances and respectfully take your leave.

Being Mindful of Those Who Have Lost a Family Member

عَنْ عَبْدِ اللَّهِ بْنِ جَعْفَرٍ ﷺ قَالَ قَالَ رَسُولُ اللَّهِ ﷺ اصْنَعُوا لِآلِ
جَعْفَرٍ طَعَامًا فَإِنَّهُ قَدْ أَتَاهُمْ أَمْرٌ شَغَلَهُمْ

'Abdullāh ibn Ja'far ﷺ narrated that the Messenger of
Allah ﷺ said: 'Prepare food for the family of Ja'far for they
have come upon an incident which has engaged them.'

Allah declares in the Qur'an: *Every soul must taste death* (*al-Anbiyā*' 21: 35). Death is an inevitable part of life. From the
moment life takes place in this world, it is on a one-way course, and its
final destination on Earth is death.

Although every human being knows death will come and there
is no escape from it, when it does eventually come, it is only natural
for family members to be shocked and deeply saddened by it. Even if
a person was ill for many months or years and everyone knows that
the person will not survive long, when death occurs, people are grief-

stricken. In the moment of grief, all other worldly affairs, be it work, business or anything else, all of it become secondary in importance and relevance. For that particular time, the priority for families becomes dealing with the death and the preparation for burial.

When Ja'far ﷺ, the brother of Ali ibn Abī Ṭālib ﷺ, died, the Prophet Muhammad ﷺ instructed his family to prepare some food for them. This is because under such circumstances, members of the household won't be up to cooking and preparing food. People are upset and sad and in no state of mind to cook.

Now, if we are supposed to go to the extent of preparing meals for families that have lost a loved one, then imagine just how important it would be to speak kind words to those families, to give them respite, and to keep an eye on their wellbeing. Following the sentiment of preparing meals for the family, we could also drop a visit once in a while, text them every now and then, and generally check up on them to show that we are there to lend a helping hand, if they need one.

This hadith teaches us that it is the duty of close family members to prepare food for the family of the deceased, and if there are no close family members then the people in the community should bring them food. This social interaction, along with all other acts of concern and support, creates a sense of care and instils companionship, love and unity for all members of the community. It instils a sense of looking out for each other and being there for one another in times of need.

26

The Blessings of Honest Trading

عَنْ عُرْوَةَ ابْنَ أَبِي الْجَعْدِ الْبَارِقِيِّ ﷺ قَالَ أَعْطَاهُ النَّبِيُّ ﷺ
دِينَارًا يَشْتَرِي بِهِ أُضْحِيَةً أَوْ شَاةً فَاشْتَرَى شَاتَيْنِ فَبَاعَ
إِحْدَاهُمَا بِدِينَارٍ فَأَتَاهُ بِشَاةٍ وَدِينَارٍ فَدَعَا لَهُ بِالْبَرَكَةِ فِي بَيْعِهِ
فَكَانَ لَوِ اشْتَرَى تُرَابًا لَرَبِحَ فِيهِ

'Urwah ibn Abū al-Ja'd al-Bāriqī ﷺ narrated that the
Prophet ﷺ gave him a dinar to buy a sacrificial animal or
a goat. He bought two goats, sold one of them for a dinar,
and returned to the Prophet ﷺ with a goat and dinar.
So, he (the Prophet ﷺ) invoked a blessing on him in his
business dealing, and he ('Urwah) was such that if had he
bought dust, he would have made a profit from it.

Buying and selling are the fabric of human society, world economy and human prosperity. It does not matter who you are, it is impossible to live life without the need to buy things. The dynamics of trade have changed from the time when it was the exchange of goods for goods (i.e., the barter system) such as 10 kg of rice for a goat, to now where goods are exchanged for money. Allah has made trading lawful, as He says: '*Allah has made trade lawful and prohibited usury*' (*al-Baqarah* 2: 275). The indispensable need for humans to buy and sell means that it needs to be regulated otherwise it is most certain that disputes and fights will break out. Exploitation is a clear taboo in the Islamic legal code of commerce. It is for this reason that interest or usury is unlawful and condemned in Islam.

This hadith teaches us some very valuable lessons. First of all, it teaches us the permissibility of appointing another person to buy and sell on our behalf. The person we appoint is called an agent or *wakīl* in Arabic. Appointing a *wakīl* also comes with rules that must be observed by both parties. One of the rules of being an agent is that the agent must carry out the instruction of the client. If he or she does not, then they will be responsible for any loss or damage caused.

However, you will notice that in this hadith, the *wakīl* of the Prophet ﷺ, 'Urwah ibn Abū al-Ja'd al-Bāriqī ﷺ, did not follow the exact instruction of the Prophet ﷺ. The Prophet ﷺ had instructed him to buy one animal for sacrifice, but 'Urwah ﷺ bought two. He then sold one for one dinar and returned to the Prophet ﷺ with one animal and one dinar. The Prophet Muhammad ﷺ was very happy with this and so, his approval proves that it is permissible for an agent to act on the best interest of the client. This type of transaction is known as *bay' al-fuḍūlī*. Once again, it should be noted that an agent must act out of the best interest of their client because if they fail to do so and are reckless, then they will be liable for any damages caused. This calls for wisdom on the part of the agent.

Finally, it is praiseworthy to pray for someone who has benefitted us. ʿUrwah al-Bāriqī's transaction was so fruitful that the Prophet Muhammad ﷺ got an animal for sacrifice without it costing him anything. This made the Prophet ﷺ invoke a special prayer for him, which teaches us to do the same in appreciation of our agent's wisdom and efforts.

୧෴୨

27

The Hide of an Animal

عَنْ ابْنِ عَبَّاسٍ ﷺ عَنْ مَيْمُونَةَ ﷺ قَالَتْ أُهْدِىَ لِمَوْلَاةٍ لَنَا شَاةٌ
مِنَ الصَّدَقَةِ فَمَاتَتْ فَمَرَّ بِهَا النَّبِيُّ ﷺ فَقَالَ أَلاَ دَبَغْتُمْ إِهَابَهَا
فَاسْتَمْتَعْتُمْ بِهِ قَالُوا يَا رَسُولَ اللهِ إِنَّهَا مَيْتَةٌ قَالَ إِنَّمَا حُرِّمَ أَكْلُهَا

Ibn ʿAbbās ﷺ said Maymūnah ﷺ said: 'A sheep was given
in alms to a female slave (*mawlāh*) of ours, but it died.
The Prophet ﷺ passed by it and said: "Why do you not
tan its skin and get some good out of it?" They replied:
"Messenger of Allah, it died a natural death." He said: "It
is only the eating of it that is prohibited."'

T he virtue of giving an animal for sacrifice is great and so is giving
an animal as a gift to the poor for them to do with it as they like.
Once, the Prophet's wife Maymūnah ﷺ gave her freed slave, termed
as *mawlāh* in Arabic, a goat as charity, because the slave's family

was among the poor. The animal was gifted with the intention that the family could either fatten it for sale or eat it. Unfortunately, the animal died and so Maymūnah ﷺ thought that no other use can be made of the animal; and since it was dead and cannot be eaten, the only option was to discard it. The Prophet Muhammad ﷺ passed by the animal and suggested they tan the skin of the animal and use it. Presuming that the Prophet ﷺ may not be aware, Maymūnah ﷺ told him that the animal had died, to which the Prophet ﷺ replied that only eating it is unlawful.

This hadith deals with the question of using animal skin, which in the modern world is used to produce many products such as shoes, bags, furniture, clothing and much more. Muslim jurists all agree that using animal skin is permissible, but they differ in the details of this. Firstly, in Islam the process of tanning can be achieved by washing, drying or any means which rid the skin of smell and decay. The great Imam Abū Ḥanīfah said that all animal skin expect for pig skin is suitable for tanning. Imam Shāfiʿī also added the skin of dogs as unsuitable hide for tanning. Imam Abū Ḥanīfah and others believed that the skin of crocodiles, snakes, monkeys, lions or any other animal is suitable to be tanned but some scholars restricted it to animals whose flesh is permissible for Muslims to eat such as sheep, cows or camels.

It is a true blessing of Allah that He has made everything on Earth for the service of humankind. Allah says: 'It is He who created for you all that is on earth' (al-Baqarah 2: 29). Animals are a blessing from Allah to us. Without animals, life on Earth would be extremely difficult. Imagine ploughing the land without animals, or carrying loads from place to place without animals, and imagine transport without animals. Animals are of great benefit to humans not only when alive but even after their death. Their skin, for instance, is usable, and if slaughtered according to Islam, their flesh is edible. Their skin provides humans with shelter from the cold and protection from the heat. In the modern world, animal skin is used to make many products, it has created jobs and is a source of business for many.

An important lesson to learn from this hadith is not to be wasteful. Allah says in the Qur'an: *'And cattle He has created for you, from them you derive warmth and numerous benefits and of their meat you eat'* (al-Naḥl 16: 5). In another verse Allah says: *'It is Allah who made your habitations homes of rest and quiet for you. He made for you out of the skins of animals, dwellings (tents), which are light (for you to carry) when you travel and when you stop. And out of their wool, fur and hair are articles of convenience for a time'* (al-Naḥl 16: 80).

Since animals provide humans with so much benefit, we have a moral obligation to care for animals, protect them from cruelty and love them. Yes, even animals understand love. Allah may have put animals on Earth to serve humankind, but it is our duty to appreciate them and our responsibility to thank Allah for them.

28

Following Protocol

عَنْ أَنَسِ بْنِ مَالِكٍ ﷺ قَالَ أَرَادَ رَسُولُ اللَّهِ ﷺ أَنْ يَكْتُبَ إِلَى
بَعْضِ الْأَعَاجِمِ فَقِيلَ لَهُ إِنَّهُمْ لاَ يَقْرَءُونَ كِتَابًا إِلاَّ بِخَاتِمٍ فَاتَّخَذَ
خَاتَمًا مِنْ فِضَّةٍ وَنَقَشَ فِيهِ   مُحَمَّدٌ رَسُولُ اللَّهِ

Anas ibn Mālik ﷺ narrates: 'The Messenger of Allah ﷺ
wanted to write to some Persian rulers. He was told that
they would not read a letter without a seal. So, the Prophet
ﷺ used a silver ring (as a seal) on which he engraved
'Muhammad the Messenger of Allah'.'

From the great signs of Allah is that He has made us of different
colour and cultures, yet our origin is one man, Adam, and one
woman, Eve. Allah says in the Qur'an: 'O mankind, indeed we have
created you from a single male and female and made you into nations
and tribes so that you may know each other' (al-Ḥujurāt 49: 13). In
another part Allah says: 'And among His signs is the creation of the

heavens and earth, and your different languages and your different (skin) colour' (*al-Rūm* 30: 22).

Culture is important because it provides humans with a sense of identity and belonging. It does not matter how poor a country is, people are still very proud of where they come from. We can see this with people who live in a different country to the one they were born in. They would still practise their culture, speak their native language and teach it to their children, and they would feed their children and guests the food of their heritage. In like manner, it is important for everyone to respect the cultural practices of others even if those practices seem strange, provided they do not break the law of Allah.

Much like society has its culture; governments and officials also have their culture of doing things. This is called procedure and protocol. This is very important because it will help people in authority determine what is authentic and what is not. The Prophet Muhammad ﷺ was doing his duty as the Messenger of Allah and inviting people to accept the message of Islam. He was unaware of the protocol of the Persians and so some of his more well-travelled Companions told him that the Persians need a particular verification that a letter is officially from the leader. If they do not have this verification, they will discard the letter without reading it. The Prophet ﷺ took this advice and got someone to make a ring which he would wear and also use as the official stamp to verify that this letter was from him.

This hadith teaches us the importance of following protocol and having our own methodology to verify what is authentic and what is not. The hadith also teaches us that taking the good practices of non-Muslim communities, provided it is not part of their religious customs, is valid and permissible. In like manner, the hadith teaches us the validity of men wearing a silver ring. We can also learn from this hadith that living in an age of Google and the internet, where a lot of information is flitting about, it is important to access information which is authentic and verified.

29

Ruqyah: *Protection from Lucky Charms and Spells*

عَنْ زَيْنَبَ امْرَأَةِ عَبْدِ اللَّهِ ﷺ عَنْ عَبْدِ اللَّهِ قَالَ سَمِعْتُ رَسُولَ
اللَّهِ ﷺ يَقُولُ إِنَّ الرُّقَى وَالتَّمَائِمَ وَالتِّوَلَةَ شِرْكٌ قَالَتْ قُلْتُ لِمَ تَقُولُ
هَذَا وَاللَّهِ لَقَدْ كَانَتْ عَيْنِي تَقْذِفُ وَكُنْتُ أَخْتَلِفُ إِلَى فُلاَنٍ
الْيَهُودِيِّ يَرْقِينِي فَإِذَا رَقَانِي سَكَنَتْ فَقَالَ عَبْدُ اللَّهِ إِنَّمَا ذَاكِ عَمَلُ
الشَّيْطَانِ كَانَ يَنْخَسُهَا بِيَدِهِ فَإِذَا رَقَاهَا كَفَّ عَنْهَا إِنَّمَا كَانَ
يَكْفِيكِ أَنْ تَقُولِي كَمَا كَانَ رَسُولُ اللَّهِ صلى الله عليه وسلم
يَقُولُ أَذْهِبِ الْبَاسَ رَبَّ النَّاسِ اشْفِ أَنْتَ الشَّافِي لاَ شِفَاءَ إِلاَّ
شِفَاؤُكَ شِفَاءً لاَ يُغَادِرُ سَقَمًا

Zaynab, the wife of ʿAbdullāh ibn Masʿūd ﷺ, narrates that ʿAbdullāh ibn Masʿūd said: 'I heard the Messenger of Allah ﷺ saying: "Spells, charms and love-potions are a form of *shirk* (polytheism)." I asked: "Why do you say this? I swear by Allah, when my eye was discharging, I used to go to so-and-so, the Jew, who performed *ruqyah* on me. When he did *ruqyah* to me, it calmed down."' 'Abdullāh said: 'That was just the work of Satan who was picking it with his hand, and when he uttered the *ruqyah* on it, he desisted. All you need to do is to say as the Messenger of Allah used to say: "Remove the harm, O Lord of men, and heal. You are the Healer. There is no remedy but Yours which leaves no disease behind."'

It is an act of disbelief and a grave sin for a person[9] to engage in black magic. It is common to hear some people saying that such-and-such object can bring them good luck. This is a form of disbelief because it entails putting faith in an object and believing it can cause them benefit or harm, while Islam teaches us that nothing can bring about good and harm except Allah.

Once the Prophet ﷺ took hold of Ibn 'Abbās ﷺ by the shoulder and told him, 'If everyone were to unite to harm you, they cannot without the Will of Allah, and if anyone wanted to benefit you, they cannot except by the Will of Allah.' Therefore, to believe that an object can harm or benefit is folly and disregarding Allah. The silly act of making love-potions to make a person fall in love with another person is equally condemned in Islam and all these acts are regarded as blasphemy and against Islam.

This hadith is interesting because it involves a discussion between 'Abdullāh ibn Mas'ūd ﷺ and his wife Zaynab ﷺ. Ibn Mas'ūd ﷺ told

---

9   Al-Tirmidhi, *Jami' al-Tirmidhi*, Hadith no. 2516

his wife that spells, charms and love-potions are polytheism, but she did not understand it, because her experience led her to appreciate the benefits of it. She told Ibn Mas'ūd ⏃ that her eye was discharging fluids and she feared it was a spell someone had cast on her. She went to a Jewish person who did *ruqyah* on her. *Ruqyah* is a form of doing something either in recitation or action with the aim to help cure an affliction whether physical or spiritual. 'Abdullāh ibn Mas'ūd ⏃ told his wife that it was better for her to seek a permanent cure rather than a temporary one and he taught her to say a supplication the Prophet ⏃ taught him:

Adh-hib al-ba's Rabb al-nās. Ishfi anta al-Shāfī lā shifā'a illā shifā'uka shifā'an lā yughādiru saqamā

This hadith teaches us a very important lesson, especially in an age when *ruqyah* has become popular, whereby people believe that only certain people can perform it and it is done in return for money. Although there is nothing wrong with someone charging for their *ruqyah* services, this hadith teaches us that anyone can do *ruqyah*, and rather than going to someone else, it would be best if one recites the supplication and blows on the affected area themself. It is hoped that by doing this a person will get better, if Allah wills.

Washing and Observing Modesty

أَنَّ رَسُولَ اللَّهِ ﷺ رَأَى رَجُلاً يَغْتَسِلُ بِالْبَرَازِ بِلاَ إِزَارٍ فَصَعِدَ الْمِنْبَرَ فَحَمِدَ اللَّهَ وَأَثْنَى عَلَيْهِ ثُمَّ قَالَ ﷺ إِنَّ اللَّهَ عَزَّ وَجَلَّ حَيٌّ سِتِّيرٌ يُحِبُّ الْحَيَاءَ وَالسَّتْرَ فَإِذَا اغْتَسَلَ أَحَدُكُمْ فَلْيَسْتَتِرْ

The Messenger of Allah ﷺ saw a man washing in a public place without a lower garment. So, he mounted the pulpit, praised and extolled Allah and said: 'Allah is characterised by modesty and concealment. So, when any of you washes, he should conceal himself.'

This is an interesting hadith which teaches us an important lesson, especially in current times, where some societies are showing liberal attitudes towards modesty. This hadith talks about a man who decided to clean himself in full public view, an extremely offensive act which violated the ethical code of Islam. It prompted the Messenger of Allah ﷺ to teach his followers the correct code of conduct. It is important to note that the Prophet ﷺ said that 'Allah is characterised by modesty and concealment' because it shows the high significance of modesty in Islam. Without being harsh towards that man, the Prophet ﷺ taught him and his followers, by extension, to cover themselves in public.

Dignity and honour are important elements for human beings, and everyone expects to be treated with respect and honour. However, these two elements need to be earned and the first way of earning respect and honour is by having a sense of self-dignity and self-honour. If a person behaves in a way that lowers their estimation in the sight of others, then they have taken steps towards losing dignity. Modesty is probably the most important factor in dignity. Allah and His Messenger ﷺ have emphasised the concept of shame and feeling shame. The reason why shame is so important is because committing sin is a shameful act and if a person does not have a sense of shame, then they will not regret the sin they have committed, and this will eventually encourage others to behave in a similar way. If a person does not regret sinning, then they will feel no remorse and if they do not feel remorse, they will not repent for their sins and therefore continue to commit sin. A sense of shame will act as a compass to guide the person to recognise their wrongdoing. Regret over the sin will make one correct themself and stop them from sinning. Without modesty, a person cannot be a true believer. The Prophet Muhammad ﷺ said, 'Modesty is a part of faith.'[10]

This hadith is important because in some societies it is considered normal for people to expose themselves and bathe or take showers with other people in nudity. For example, in sports centres, some people take showers naked in the presence of other people. This is not allowed in Islam, nor is it permissible to share the shower area with people who have exposed themselves.

Modesty will bring us close to Allah; without it, a person cannot get close to Allah.

---

10 Al-Bukhari, *Sahih al-Bukhari,* Hadith no. 9

Having Pictures and Dogs in the House

عَنْ أَبِى طَلْحَةَ الأَنْصَارِيِّ ﷺ قَالَ سَمِعْتُ النَّبِيَّ ﷺ يَقُولُ لاَ
تَدْخُلُ الْمَلاَئِكَةَ بَيْتًا فِيهِ كَلْبٌ وَلاَ تِمْثَالٌ

Abū Ṭalḥah al-Anṣārī ﷺ narrated: 'I heard the Prophet
ﷺ say: "The angels do not enter a house which contains a
dog or statues."'

W hen Saʿīd ibn Yāsar al-Anṣārī ﷺ transmitted this hadith, Zayd
ibn Khālid al-Juhanī ﷺ wanted verification and so he said to
him: 'Come with me to ʿĀ'ishah, so that we ask her about it.' They
went and said to her: 'Mother of Believers, Abū Ṭalḥāh has transmitted
to us a hadith. Have you heard the Prophet ﷺ mentioning that?' She
replied: 'No, but I will tell you what I saw him doing. The Messenger of
Allah ﷺ went on an expedition and I was waiting for his return. I got a
carpet which I hung as a screen on a stick over the door. When he came,
I received him and said: "Peace be upon you, Messenger of Allah, His
mercy and His blessings. Praise be to Allah who gave you dominance

and respect." Then he looked at the house and saw the carpet; and he did not respond to me at all. I found (signs of) disapproval on his face. He then came to the carpet and tore it down. He then said: "Allah has not commanded us to clothe stones and clay out of what He has given us."' She said: 'I then cut it to pieces and made two pillows out of it and stuffed them with palm fibre, and he did not disapprove of that.'

Evil does not spread instantly and overnight, rather it is slow and insidious. In a lot of cases, evil starts off as an innocent act or a minor event only to grow and develop into a major problem. Perhaps pictures and making statues is a good example to prove this point. It is believed that during previous nations, pictures and making idols were allowed. When important people would pass away some people would make statues and images to commemorate them. Through the passage of time, later generations started to believe that these statues have powers and can grant wishes, bring them closer to God and answer prayers. This then eventually turned into accepting them as gods.

Islam is clear regarding its stance with pictures and statues. Animate objects are not allowed to be drawn or statues made of them. This is an important message for Muslims to note and practise by making sure that our houses are free of pictures and statues of animate objects. Islam has also prohibited us from raising dogs in our houses, unless it is for the reason of guidance or protection.

This hadith teaches Muslims the prohibition of having pictures and dogs in the house. This hadith also teaches an important lesson about clarifying the authenticity of any news. The Prophet's Companions wanted to clarify the hadith so they went and asked the Prophet's wife 'Ā'ishah ﷺ if she can confirm the hadith. Although she could not confirm the exact words of the hadith, she did relate a story which provides a similar meaning.

The reaction of 'Ā'ishah ﷺ when she noticed the Prophet's disapproval is important to note. When she realised that the Prophet ﷺ was irritated, she immediately proceeded to resolve the issue. This is because Muslims are commanded to obey the Prophet Muhammad ﷺ, and ʿĀʾishah ◈ has shown us by example how the Prophet ﷺ ought to be obeyed. If the Prophet ﷺ dislikes something and we continue to do it, are we really obeying him and respecting his teachings? Being able to sacrifice our desires, no matter how tough it may be to do so, just to follow the Prophet ﷺ is true obedience to him and complete submission to Allah.

Never Refuse Perfume

عَنْ أَبِي هُرَيْرَةَ ﷺ قَالَ قَالَ رَسُولُ اللهِ ﷺ مَنْ عُرِضَ عَلَيْهِ طِيبٌ
فَلاَ يَرُدَّهُ فَإِنَّهُ طَيِّبُ الرِّيحِ خَفِيفُ الْمَحْمَلِ

Abū Hurayrah ﷺ reported the Messenger of Allah ﷺ as
saying: 'If anyone is presented with perfume, he should
not reject it, for it is a thing of good fragrance and light
to bear.'

Allah has created human beings to be attracted to things which are
nice and pleasant, and that is why we instinctively dislike things
which are nasty and unpleasant. For example, if a food item is presented
nicely, it attracts the person to eat it. That is why shops and restaurants
spend a lot of time displaying the food in a captivating way. The same is
true with all shops trying to sell their products to people.

Smell is one of the most powerful ways of getting our attention. If
a restaurant were to smell unpleasant, it is most likely that people will

turn away from it. Smell incites the imagination and is very important for our sensory pleasure and experience. Due to the power of smell, the Prophet Muhammad ﷺ has prohibited women from wearing perfume around strange men as it will draw their attention towards her, which goes against the precepts of observing the hijab.

Smell is important in our daily interaction with other people. Islam has emphasised much on personal hygiene and encouraged people to bathe and wash regularly. Special emphasis is placed on days where the masses gather such as the Friday Prayer and the Eid Prayer. The Prophet Muhammad ﷺ has told people to keep away from the mosques until they have removed any odour on them.

Using perfume is one way of enhancing the positive aroma emitted from a person. Islam encourages people to apply perfume in order to smell good. In many cultures, it is customary to offer friends and guests perfume as a way of showing hospitality, kindness and friendship. This hadith teaches us to take any opportunity where perfume is given. Not only does it show the appreciation of the recipient of the perfume to the giver of the perfume, but it will also help a person to smell good. This is an easy way of observing a Sunnah of the Prophet Muhammad ﷺ.

It is worth noting that during the time of the Prophet ﷺ, perfume was extracted in a pure and sanitised way, but in today's world perfume is mixed with many chemicals. Some people may be allergic to these substances and therefore if they refuse perfume for this reason, then they will have not acted against the Sunnah.

The Rights of the Road

عَنْ أَبِي سَعِيدٍ الْخُدْرِيِّ ﷺ أَنَّ رَسُولَ اللَّهِ ﷺ قَالَ إِيَّاكُمْ
وَالْجُلُوسَ بِالطُّرُقَاتِ فَقَالُوا يَا رَسُولَ اللَّهِ مَا بُدُّ لَنَا مِنْ مَجَالِسِنَا
نَتَحَدَّثُ فِيهَا فَقَالَ رَسُولُ اللَّهِ ﷺ إِنْ أَبَيْتُمْ فَأَعْطُوا الطَّرِيقَ
حَقَّهُ قَالُوا وَمَا حَقُّ الطَّرِيقِ يَا رَسُولَ اللَّهِ قَالَ غَضُّ الْبَصَرِ وَكَفُّ
الأَذَى وَرَدُّ السَّلاَمِ وَالأَمْرُ بِالْمَعْرُوفِ وَالنَّهْيُ عَنِ الْمُنْكَرِ

Abū Saʿīd al-Khudrī ﷺ reported the Messenger of Allah
ﷺ as saying: 'Avoid sitting on the roads.' The people said:
'Messenger of Allah! We must have meeting places in
which to converse.' The Messenger of Allah ﷺ said: 'If
you insist on meeting, give the road its due.' They asked:
'What is the due of roads, O Messenger of Allah?' He
replied: 'Lowering the eyes, avoiding anything offensive,

returning salutation, commanding what is reputable and
forbidding what is disreputable.'

It is amazing how much detail the Prophet Muhammad ﷺ has
taught his followers about life, trying to enhance their character and
raise their standards by teaching them the optimal way of behaving.
There are some things which are categorically wrong and those are
forbidden, and then there are other things which are clearly lawful
and good to do. Those will take you closer to Allah and get you into
Paradise. However, there arises a question regarding things which are
lawful to do: Just because they are lawful to do, does this always mean
that we can do them? Let us take for example, building an extension to
our houses. The Qur'an and Sunnah of the Prophet Muhammad ﷺ do
not prohibit it, therefore it is lawful; but does it mean that a person can
make an extension on their house, regardless of it causing harm to their
neighbours? The answer is no. Just because something might be lawful
does not mean that it is the best thing to do.

Behaving in the optimal manner is always the wise thing to do,
such as waiting your turn in the queue and not pushing in. That is to
say, lining up in a queue is not a requirement in Islam and pushing
in the queue is not unlawful in Islam, but pushing in the queue *does*
violate good manners of behaviour. Therefore, a Muslim cannot say
that since Islam does not prohibit jumping the queue, we can do it.
The primary lesson this hadith teaches is the importance of behaving
in the most optimal manner.

During the time of the Prophet ﷺ, it was a common practice for
people to meet and discuss issues or even chat. The ideal place to gather
was by the roads, perhaps because the ground was beaten and firm so
sitting on it was better. Traffic in terms of animals and caravans using
the road in those times was not as intense as it is today. Sitting on the
road meant that others could easily join in and the meeting place would

be known. The Prophet 🌸 wanted to teach his followers the right etiquettes about this practice.

He did not say 'Do not sit on the roads,' rather he said, 'Beware of sitting on the roads.' His Companions replied that they needed a place to socialise, meet and chat. The Prophet 🌸 then told them if they want to meet up at the roads then they must observe the etiquettes or rights of the road. They were confused as to what the 'rights' of the roads were, so they asked the Prophet 🌸 to explain. The Prophet 🌸 then listed out the main etiquettes.

Firstly, he spoke about lowering the gaze. This means that when women are passing by, one must resist the temptation to look or stare at them. It is immodest to do that. It causes the hearts to be stirred up with wrong emotions and would make road users feel uncomfortable.

Secondly, the Prophet 🌸 told them to avoid causing others any harm, such as littering or leaving behind debris. His instructions meant they should clean up after themselves and avoid blocking the path or speaking badly about those passing by.

Thirdly, people gathering for social purposes must be mindful to return the greetings of *salām* and not be distracted by their conversations. Finally, they must not forget to tell people to do good, and if they see something wrong, they must stop it.

These are the rights of using the road. Although this was said to people over 1400 years ago, we can see how this still applies to our lives today.

❦

34

Natural Characteristics of People

عَنْ أَبِي هُرَيْرَةَ ۞ يَبْلُغُ بِهِ النَّبِيَّ ۞ الْفِطْرَةُ خَمْسٌ أَوْ خَمْسٌ
مِنَ الْفِطْرَةِ الْخِتَانُ وَالاِسْتِحْدَادُ وَنَتْفُ الإِبْطِ وَتَقْلِيمُ الأَظْفَارِ
وَقَصُّ الشَّارِبِ

Abū Hurayrah ۞ narrated the Prophet ۞ as saying:
'Five things are of the inborn characteristics of man:
circumcision, shaving the pubic hair, plucking the armpit
hair, clipping the nails, and trimming the moustache.'

*'By the fig and the olive. And by Mount Sinai. And by this city
(of Makkah) a haven of peace. Surely, We have created man in the
best mould' (al-Tīn 95: 1–4).*

B lessed is Allah the best of creators who has created everything
with a purpose and benefit. There can be little doubt that from
among all living creatures, human beings enjoy a high level of marvel

in terms of their creation. It is this high level of creation which Allah has endowed with honour and dignity. Whilst it is true that Allah has created humankind with many strengths, He has also created them with weaknesses.

Humans are living creatures and their physiological build means that they develop differently from angels and jinns. Like all other creatures we can see around us, humans go through different phases from birth to death. One common factor all animals share is growth. However, unlike other animals, humans have the unique position of being Allah's representative on Earth. As such, Allah has commanded people to maintain a particular image and presentation. This is so important that Allah has made it a natural instinct of man.

Circumcision helps to keep the private area of men clean and free from infection, and it helps a person to wash himself better. The removal of pubic hair from around the groin area and the armpits is to ensure hygiene and amplify human beauty. The overgrowth of bodily hair can be repulsive, and it can be unpleasant when in a state of intimacy between husband and wife. The removal of bodily hair therefore presents humans in a much more attractive way.

Long nails attract dirt and germs to gather and collect therein. When nails grow too long, it presents a bad image of that person. Moreover, long nails are associated with claws and claws are associated with animals. Humans must be distinct from animals. It may be a fashion trend in some places to have long nails painted with bright colours and beautiful patterns, but this goes against the teachings of Islam. It is meaningless and wrong to spend so much time and money on this, especially when they could be used for more fruitful activities.

Hair is an excellent agent to attract dirt, and moustaches are most susceptible to smears and stains. Overgrown moustaches also make a person look shabby and unkempt. This is the reason why Allah has made it such that man naturally inclines towards trimming these hairs in order to look nice and better presented.

Essentially, these articles are related to personal hygiene which fits into the overall ethos of Islam about cleanliness, purification, and beautification. It is the natural and complete way in which Allah created mankind. Whether society or the environment has influenced man to behave differently are factors for other consideration, but Muslims must adhere to observing these acts of personal hygiene and grooming. The Prophet Muhammad ﷺ advised that pubic and armpit hair should be removed at least once within forty days.[11] However, this may differ from person to person depending on how quickly one's hair grows. Being presentable and appearing and smelling nice play an important role in developing a positive attitude in people and this in turn, builds confidence. That is why it is important for Muslims to make sure that these five basic acts of grooming are followed.

〜

---

11   Abu Dawud, *Sunan Abu Dawud*, Hadith no. 4196

35

Wind: The Mercy from Allah

وعن أبي هريرة ﷺ قال سمعت رسول الله ﷺ يقول الريح من
روح الله تأتي بالرحمة وتأتي بالعذاب فإذا رأيتموها فلا تسبوها
وسلوا الله خيرها واستعيذوا بالله من شرها

Abū Hurayrah ﷺ said: 'I heard the Messenger of Allah
ﷺ saying: "The wind is the blessing of Allah. Sometimes
it brings His mercy and sometimes it brings His
chastisement. When you experience strong wind do not
revile it but ask Allah for its good; and seek Allah's refuge
against its evil."'

*'Allah created the seven heavens one upon another. You will see no
inconsistency in the Merciful One's creation. Turn your vision again,
can you see any flaws? Then turn your vision again, and then again;
in the end your vision will come back to you, worn out and frustrated'*
(al-Mulk 67: 1–4).

The remarkable Words of Allah ring true and cannot be denied. Allah has created this world in perfection. Its equilibrium amplifies the Majesty of Allah. Let's stop to ponder the perfect and precise atmospheric pressure to sustain life. The pull of gravity is just perfect to keep objects on the ground. Similarly, the oxygen level is balanced to help all living things breathe. If the balance is disturbed, it would create devastation. The sun is placed at an optimal position; if it were too close, the planet would heat up too much to sustain life, and if it were too far, the planet would be too cold to sustain life. The ecological system works in harmony to help life on Earth to continue and provide sustenance for all living creatures. We can go on and on talking about the marvel of this world and how it sustains life. This in itself is a proof of Allah's Majesty, Splendour and Grandeur.

One such creation of Allah is the wind. The wind is a natural element which is vital to sustain life on Earth. Wind helps control global temperature, pollination, carry ships from country to country, and much more. Although Allah has created the winds for the benefit of His creation, if His creation reaches a level of disobedience and transgression beyond toleration, then Allah can send these natural phenomena to chastise humankind and bring them back to the Straight Path.

The nation of 'Ād is a good example of how people disobeyed Allah and transgressed Allah's Law to an extent that the only recourse was to destroy those people. Allah says: *'The Thamūd and the 'Ād denied the (possibility of a) sudden calamity, calling it false. Then the Thamūd were destroyed by an awesome upheaval. And 'Ād were destroyed by a furiously raging windstorm which He let loose upon them for seven nights and days in succession; so that (if you had been there) you might have seen people lying prostrate, as though they were uprooted trunks of hollow palm trees'* (al-Ḥāqqah 69: 4–7).

In this hadith, the Prophet ﷺ teaches Muslims that the wind is a mercy from Allah. The reason why it is a mercy is because life on Earth will not be possible without the wind, so the purpose of wind is to serve humankind. However, if need be, Allah can also turn it into a weapon to chastise humans such as in the case of the nation of 'Ād.

Strong winds can be terrifying and can cause stress to humans. When humans are scared or annoyed, they tend to insult the source of their fear. The Prophet Muhammad ﷺ taught us not to do that, but instead to seek refuge in Allah and ask Him for a beneficial wind.

☙

36

Sending Greetings upon the Prophet Muhammad ﷺ

عَنْ أَبِى هُرَيْرَةَ ﷺ قَالَ قَالَ رَسُولُ اللَّهِ ﷺ لاَ تَجْعَلُوا بُيُوتَكُمْ قُبُورًا وَلاَ تَجْعَلُوا قَبْرِى عِيدًا وَصَلُّوا عَلَىَّ فَإِنَّ صَلاَتَكُمْ تَبْلُغُنِى حَيْثُ كُنْتُمْ

Abū Hurayrah ﷺ narrated that the Messenger of Allah ﷺ said: 'Do not make your houses graves, and do not make my grave a place of festivity. But invoke greetings on me, for your greetings reach me wherever you may be.'

'Indeed Allah and His angels send greetings to His Prophet. O you who believe, send your greetings to him and salute him with all respect' (*al-Aḥzāb* 33: 56).

The high status of the Prophet Muhammad ﷺ is shown by the fact that Allah Himself sends His greetings to the Prophet Muhammad ﷺ; not only that but He has commanded His angels to do the same.

Allah's love for the Prophet Muhammad ﷺ can be seen clearly in the verse stated above. This is a unique station of love, honour and tribute for the Prophet Muhammad ﷺ. If Allah and His angels send greetings upon the Prophet Muhammad ﷺ, then it is more worthy that the followers of Muhammad ﷺ should send greetings upon their Prophet ﷺ too.

Sending greetings to the Prophet ﷺ is a highly virtuous deed, so much so that Allah has instructed Muslims to include it during their five daily prayers. Beyond that, Muslims should always send greeting to the Prophet Muhammad ﷺ whenever they can. In another hadith, the Prophet ﷺ told us, whoever sends greetings upon him once, Allah will send greetings upon them tenfold.[12] In reference to the afore-cited Qur'anic verse, a man came to the Prophet Muhammad ﷺ and asked him how he should send greetings to him. The Prophet Muhammad ﷺ taught him the salutations we recite when sitting down in prayer. A shorter and simpler way a person can send greetings to the Prophet Muhammad ﷺ is to say, '*Allāhumma ṣallī 'alā Muhammad*'. It takes two seconds to say it, but the virtue of it is great.

In this hadith, there are two main things the Prophet ﷺ wanted to teach us, and in order to do so he gave the example of a grave. Generally, one of two things happen at graves; they are either abandoned and forsaken with little to no visitors, or they become a place of visitation, gathering and celebration.

Regarding the first lesson, when the Prophet ﷺ told Muslims not to turn their homes into a grave, what he meant was that men must pray the voluntary prayers at home and not stick to praying only in the mosque. When a person prays at home, Allah sends His blessing upon that home and the angels visit it because Allah's Name is mentioned. When there is no mention of Allah's Name, then the blessings of Allah do not descend. Therefore, it becomes empty, abandoned and forsaken.

---

12 Muslim, *Sahih Muslim*, Hadith no. 384

Similarly, the one who does not remember Allah is like the one who is dead, hence their home will be like a graveyard full of dead people.

The second part of the hadith is also very important. It seems to be a practice in many nations and cultures to commemorate the dead. When the deceased is a very important person, the desire some humans have to remember and revere them increases by many folds. So, people sometimes end up making the graves of the dead sacred, by decorating them, holding acts of celebrations, praying therein and holding superstitious beliefs about them. The Prophet Muhammad ﷺ warned his followers of falling into this trap like the Jews and the Christians did, and instructed them not to make his grave into a place of celebrations and falsehood. His grave can be visited, and people can send their greetings to him in front of his grave, but that is the extent of what is lawful and permissible to do. It should be noted that unholy acts or prayer and statements should be avoided, because it is sinful and of no benefit to the person or the Prophet Muhammad ﷺ.

People must be calm and respectful when visiting the Prophet's grave. The best thing a person can do is to recite greetings to the Prophet ﷺ, because he receives the greetings we send him.

37

Swearing at Time

عَنْ أَبِي هُرَيْرَةَ ﷺ عَنِ النَّبِيِّ ﷺ يَقُولُ اللَّهُ عَزَّ وَجَلَّ يُؤْذِينِي ابْنُ
آدَمَ يَسُبُّ الدَّهْرَ وَأَنَا الدَّهْرُ بِيَدِيَ الأَمْرُ أُقَلِّبُ اللَّيْلَ وَالنَّهَارَ

Abū Hurayrah ﷺ reported the Prophet ﷺ as saying:
'Allah Most High says: "The son of Adam injures Me
by abusing time, whereas I am time. Authority is in My
Hand. I alternate the night and the day."'

*'And they say: There is nothing but our life of this world, we die and we
live and nothing destroys us except al-Dahr (time)' (al-Jāthiyah 45: 24).*

This hadith is known as a *Hadith Qudsī*. This means that Allah said
this to the Prophet ﷺ and the Prophet ﷺ expressed it in his own
words. Therefore, this is a special hadith because it contains the Words
of Allah unlike other ahadith which are the words of the Prophet
Muhammad ﷺ inspired by Allah.

This is an important hadith for everyone to pay attention to and it is complicated to understand, because the meaning is unclear as to how Allah is time and how an insult to time is an insult to Allah. The great hadith scholar Imam al-Nawawī provides an invaluable explanation to this hadith. He says that 'insulting time' is a metaphor the Arabs used when disasters such as death, old age, or loss of money occurred. The meaning of the phrase 'Allah is time' means that Allah is the One who causes those events and accidents to happen, and He is the Creator of all that happens.

The pre-Islamic Arabs would say, 'Woe to time' and other phrases cursing or castigating time. This is un-Islamic, and the Prophet ﷺ instructed his followers to refrain from saying such a thing. What is meant by 'Do not curse time for Allah is time' is 'Do not castigate the One who brings about those disasters, for that will be directed towards Allah, for He is the One who causes them to happen.' This is because *dahr* means *waqt* (time) which cannot do anything on its own. Rather, since time has been created by Allah, insulting time would mean indirectly insulting Allah. Ibn Kathīr records similar views from al-Shāfiʿī and Abū ʿUbaydah Qasim ibn Sallam.[13] In their commentary of this hadith, they said that during the pre-Islamic age, if some difficulty, trial or disaster befell the Arabs, they would say 'Woe to time', attributing those events to time and denouncing time.

Time is measured by the alternation of night and day. The phrase, 'It is in My Hand, I alternate the night and the day' is to emphasise the fact that time is not an independent entity but a creation of Allah which He controls. Therefore, swearing at time is not really swearing at time but an insult to Allah Most High, the Creator of time.

Some scholars interpreted the hadith to mean wasting time. By wasting time, humans insult time and thereby Allah, because time is a very special gift given to people from Allah. However, the first interpretation is the more common one amongst the scholars.

---

13 Al-Mubarakpuri, *ʿAwn al-Maʿbud*, Vol. 14, p. 152

38

Be Good to People Despite How They Are

عَنْ عَائِشَةَ ﷺ قَالَتِ اسْتَأْذَنَ رَجُلٌ عَلَى النَّبِيِّ ﷺ فَقَالَ بِئْسَ
ابْنُ الْعَشِيرَةِ أَوْ بِئْسَ رَجُلُ الْعَشِيرَةِ ثُمَّ قَالَ ائْذَنُوا لَهُ فَلَمَّا دَخَلَ
أَلَانَ لَهُ الْقَوْلَ فَقَالَتْ عَائِشَةُ يَا رَسُولَ اللَّهِ أَلَنْتَ لَهُ الْقَوْلَ وَقَدْ
قُلْتَ لَهُ مَا قُلْتَ قَالَ إِنَّ شَرَّ النَّاسِ عِنْدَ اللَّهِ مَنْزِلَةً يَوْمَ الْقِيَامَةِ
مَنْ وَدَعَهُ أَوْ تَرَكَهُ النَّاسُ لِاتِّقَاءِ فُحْشِهِ

'Ā'ishah ﷺ said: 'A man asked permission to see the Prophet ﷺ, and he said: "He is a bad son of the tribe," or "He is a bad member of the tribe." He then said: "Give him permission." Then when he entered, he spoke to him leniently.' 'Ā'ishah then asked: 'Apostle of Allah! You spoke to him leniently while you said about him what you said!' He replied: 'The one with the worst position in

Allah's estimation on the Day of Resurrection will be the one whom people left alone for fear of his rudeness.'

The commentator of the Qur'an, Jalāl al-Dīn al-Maḥallī mentions the story of Adam's creation. He narrates that when Allah commanded the angels to collect earth to create Adam, the angels collected it from seventy different parts of the globe. The quality of earth is not the same. There is soil where the crops flourish and are healthy and with little care and tilling, it produces good crops; and some soil, no matter how much you do to it, it does not produce anything. Humankind is created from earth and in similar fashion to soil, some people are good, some are in between, and some are bad.

Once a man who was known to be wicked came to visit the Prophet Muhammad ﷺ. He knocked on the door of the Prophet ﷺ and when the Prophet ﷺ saw him, he said with disapproval to his wife 'Ā'ishah ؚ, that he is a bad member of the tribe. The Prophet ﷺ, nevertheless, welcomed the man in and dealt with him in a gracious manner. 'Ā'ishah ؚ was surprised at the way the Prophet ﷺ dealt with him despite what he has said about him. The Prophet ﷺ took that opportunity to teach 'Ā'ishah ؚ that the person who will have the worst position in Allah's estimation on the Day of Judgement will be the one whom people left alone for fear of his bad traits. In another hadith the Prophet ﷺ said, 'Allah does not like the one who is foul and lewd in his language.'

There are two angles to the lessons we can take from this hadith. Firstly, the Prophet ﷺ entertained the man despite his bad traits. He did not ignore him even though that would have been easier to do. We can see just how noble this gesture is when the Prophet ﷺ followed up this incident with the information that the one with the worst position in Allah's estimation on the Day of Resurrection will be the one whom people left alone for fear of his rudeness. Meaning, if a person is ignored by the people due to his rude behaviour, he stands to occupy the worst position in Allah's Sight on the Last Day. We do not even remotely want to become the reason for someone else's doom in the Hereafter, and so we should pay heed to people even if they are known to be wicked, and give them our time and attention when they seek it. This is a profound way of looking at this hadith, and one which would grant us a high status in Allah's Sight, by the Will of Allah.

Secondly, through this hadith, the Prophet ﷺ is warning us to avoid becoming the worst people on the Day of Judgement. The bad behaviour of some people towards us does not give us the license to behave towards them in a similar manner. What is interesting in this hadith is that when the Prophet ﷺ let the man enter into his house, he didn't just speak to him, but he did so leniently and politely. He spoke to him with excellence. This teaches us that we should always maintain the highest standard of dealing with people. Once a Bedouin came to the Prophet Muhammad ﷺ and tugged on his clothing so hard that it made a mark on his neck.[14] Yet the Prophet ﷺ did not shout at him, rather he listened to what he had to say. This was the character of the Prophet Muhammad ﷺ; benevolent, noble and pious. It is his character that we must aim to emulate, regardless of the behaviour of those around us.

ༀ

---

14 Al-Bukhari, *Sahih al-Bukhari*, Hadith no. 6088

How the Prophet ﷺ Dealt with People on a Personal Level

عَنْ أَنَسٍ ﷺ قَالَ مَا رَأَيْتُ رَجُلاً الْتَقَمَ أُذُنَ رَسُولِ اللَّهِ ﷺ
فَيُنَحِّى رَأْسَهُ حَتَّى يَكُونَ الرَّجُلُ هُوَ الَّذِى يُنَحِّى رَأْسَهُ وَمَا رَأَيْتُ
رَجُلاً أَخَذَ بِيَدِهِ فَتَرَكَ يَدَهُ حَتَّى يَكُونَ الرَّجُلُ هُوَ الَّذِى يَدَعُ يَدَهُ

Anas ibn Mālik ﷺ narrated: 'I never saw that when any
man brought his mouth to the ear of the Messenger of
Allah ﷺ and he withdrew his head until the man himself
withdrew his head, and I never saw that when any man
took him by his hand and he withdrew his hand, until the
man himself withdrew his hand.'

The Prophet Muhammad ﷺ was known as a gentle man with
impeccable manners and a benign code of conduct. He always
spent time with people and listened to their problems, offered advice
and prayed for them. This hadith is one of many that teach us the way

the Prophet ﷺ would interact with people. Anas ibn Mālik ؓ narrates that if someone came to meet the Prophet ﷺ and wanted to speak to him quietly and privately, he would lower his ears so the person could speak and he would remain in that position until the person had finished and moved his mouth away from the ear of the Prophet ﷺ. In like manner, the Prophet ﷺ would not remove his hand from someone who had taken his hands until the person themself released the Prophet's hand. This was the gentle nature of the Prophet Muhammad ﷺ. It shows his caring and kind way of dealing with people.

The reason why the Prophet ﷺ did not pull his head back from a person speaking to him is because doing so shows signs of frustration and not caring to listen to what the person has to say. Similarly, when a person is holding his hand, he did not pull it away in fear of upsetting the person holding his hands.

This hadith teaches us that if a person extends their hand to shake, then we should be patient until that person lets go first and we should try not to pull our hand away. In like manner, if a person is having a conversation with us, we should listen to them until they have finished saying what they want to say.

This hadith also shows us the gracious way in which the Prophet ﷺ dealt with people. If the cultural practice of any place differs from this, then there is no harm in a person behaving according to that custom. The important thing to note is to be friendly to people and treat them with respect.

❦

Control Your Anger

عَنْ عَبْدِ اللهِ بن مسعود ﷺ قَالَ قَالَ رَسُولُ اللهِ ﷺ مَا تَعُدُّونَ
الصُّرَعَةَ فِيكُمْ قَالُوا الَّذِى لاَ يَصْرَعُهُ الرِّجَالُ قَالَ لاَ وَلَكِنَّهُ الَّذِى
يَمْلِكُ نَفْسَهُ عِنْدَ الْغَضَبِ

'Abdullāh ibn Mas'ūd ﷺ reported the Messenger of Allah
ﷺ as saying: 'Who do you consider a wrestler among you?'
The people replied: 'A man whom the men cannot defeat
in wrestling.' He said: 'No, it is he who controls himself
when he is angry.'

Glory be to Allah who has created humankind and fashioned them
in the best mould. Praise be to Allah who has created humankind
with emotions. It is these emotions that make humankind react with
sympathy, compassion and care for those in need. Our emotions are
what make us react to injustice, but sometimes our emotions can lead
us to act in an unfriendly way.

Anger is a human response to something we find upsetting or annoying. Every human has the capacity to get angry and everyone in some part of their life will get angry. Sometimes anger can be a healthy thing. When something wrong has happened, reacting with appropriate anger helps to show others our disapproval. This is a praiseworthy anger. At times, the Prophet ﷺ would be annoyed, and he expressed his disapproval in an angry tone. He never screamed or shouted at people, but his disapproval was visible from his facial expressions.

Anger that is disapproved is that which is overly aggressive, that which leads to shouting and screaming, and quickly getting angry with people over minor issues. This type of anger leads to ill feelings, and more dangerously, when anger leads to aggression, it can create an aggressive response. This can then easily spiral into confrontation, fighting and worse. It is one of the worst situations to be in, because anger blinds a person and makes people say things which they later regret. Unfortunately, by the time the person realises their blunder, it is too late, because words cannot be taken back and 'sorry' only goes so far to heal the wounds of the words that were spoken. Once a man, known for his temper, came to the Prophet ﷺ and asked him for advice. The Prophet ﷺ told him, 'Do not get angry.'[15] The man repeated his request for advice and the Prophet ﷺ said nothing to him other than repeating his advice about controlling his anger.

The Prophet Muhammad ﷺ was always gentle in his approach to people. Perhaps this famous hadith of Anas ؓ best illustrates the exceptional conduct of the Prophet ﷺ and his ability to control his anger. Anas ؓ narrates that he served the Prophet ﷺ for about ten years and within that time he never shouted at him or showed frustration for something he did or something he did not do. Imagine serving someone for ten years and never hearing them shout at you or

---

15 Al-Tirmidhi, *Jami' al-Tirmidhi*, Hadith no. 2020, Al-Bukhari and others.

even show frustration! Anas 🍃 went on to say that the Prophet 🕌 had the best character.

Anger is extremely difficult to control and once it rises it is *almost impossible* to control the outburst. But it is not impossible. It requires training and self-discipline to control anger. It is interesting to note how the Prophet 🕌 taught his followers about anger and controlling it by giving the example of a wrestler. Just like wrestling, controlling anger when it rises takes every ounce of effort and strength. In fact, wrestling is easier than controlling anger.

The Prophet Muhammad 🕌 has also taught Muslims how to control anger. He told us: 'I know a phrase which by repeating it, one could get rid of his angry feelings: "I seek refuge in Allah from the accursed devil" (*a'ūdhu billāhi min al-shaytān al-rajīm*).'[16] He also taught us that when one of us becomes angry while standing, they should sit down. If the anger leaves, it is all well and good; otherwise, they should lie down.[17]

჻჻჻

---

16 Sulayman ibn Surad said: "I was sitting with the Prophet (peace and blessings of Allah be upon him), and two men were slandering one another. One of them was red in the face, and the veins on his neck were standing out. The Prophet (peace and blessings of Allah be upon him) said, 'I know a word which, if he were to say it, what he feels would go away. If he said "I seek refuge with Allah from the Satan," what he feels would go away.' Abu Dawud, *Sunan Abu Dawud*, Hadith no. 4773

17 Abu Dawud, *Sunan Abu Dawud*, Hadith no. 4782